It's been said that mentoring is [...] while discipleship is "Come and do life with me." When it comes to the latter, there is no better person to attach our lives to and be apprenticed by than Jesus Christ. Sorry; no celebrity Christian leader will suffice as a surrogate substitute. This is the point my friend Pastor Robert Gelinas excavates profoundly in this highly accessible book, *Discipled by Jesus*. I pray this gets a wide reading for generations to come!

BRYAN LORITTS, senior pastor, Abundant Life Christian Fellowship, author of *Saving the Saved*

Robert Gelinas is revolutionizing everything we have ever known about discipleship. A clarion call to pursue a life of faith that is richer and deeper than we had ever imagined.

MANDY ARIOTO, president and CEO, MOPS International

A treasure chest filled with spiritual wisdom. This book is a much-needed course correction for the people of God. With so much religion around, Robert keeps pointing us back to Jesus.

DANIEL FUSCO, author of *Upward, Inward, Outward* and *Honestly*

One of the most exciting teaching pastors in the world invites God's church to welcome Jesus himself back to the exclusive role of making his own disciples—because nobody but Jesus can. As African American believers have sung for decades, "Can't nobody do me like Jesus!" For a church gone dry, Robert steps forth to offer its best teacher, discipler, and leader: the living Christ. Dynamic, urgent, and inviting.

> **PATRICIA RAYBON,** author of *I Told the Mountain to Move* and *My First White Friend*

Skillfully exposes some of the myths underlying the way many of us have thought of discipleship and then compassionately leads us to a vibrant walk of faith with the risen Christ. This book not only changed the way I think about discipleship; it changed the way I live as a disciple.

> **MARK S. YOUNG,** president, Denver Seminary

Robert Gelinas, my pastor, hand-delivers Jesus' invitation: *Come. Follow Me. I will make you disciples.* Wait no more. Read on and discover all that is waiting for you when you accept the invitation to be discipled by Jesus.

> **ELISA MORGAN,** speaker, author of *The Beauty of Broken* and *Hello, Beauty Full*

A powerful book that grasps the reality of Jesus being the one who transforms us!

> **JOHN H. SATHER,** co-national director, Cru Inner City

I hadn't even made it through the introduction before my "steady as she goes" Christian journey started getting rocked. With a thoughtful spotlight on Scripture, *Discipled by Jesus* unwraps this beautiful and compelling reality: I can be discipled by the Messiah himself.

> **DAN WOLGEMUTH,** president and CEO, Youth For Christ USA

Finally, a book on discipleship that invites readers not to know more, to do more, to be more, or to give more to Jesus, but simply and significantly to be with Jesus.

DR. MARK DEYMAZ, author of *Disruption: Repurposing the Church to Redeem the Community*

This book is not simply a shift in language; it's a call to encounter the risen Christ.

SCOTT LUNDEEN, program director, iSSACHAR Center for Urban Leadership

Robert Gelinas has done it again. I am touched by God every time I sit under his teaching. This book is liberating me in ministry and inspiring me to re-enroll in the school where Christ is the teacher.

TYLER JOHNSON, lead pastor of Redemption AZ

A prophetic pronouncement to all who want a fresh encounter with the resurrected Christ and the promised Holy Spirit.

BRADY BOYD, New Life Church, Colorado Springs, author of *Addicted to Busy* and *Speak Life*

Once again, the Jazz Theologian has delivered. Robert Gelinas connects disciple-making with the ongoing journey of deepening our intimacy with and identity in Christ.

EFREM SMITH, co-lead pastor of Bayside Church Midtown, author of *Killing Us Softly: Reborn in the Upside-Down Image of God*

Gelinas invites us to run down a road toward a discipleship revolution with him. In these pages he challenges our paradigms as he reminds us of the winsome love of Jesus. Ingest this book!

ALAN BRIGGS, pastor, coach, consultant, author of *Everyone's a Genius*, *Guardrails*, and *Staying Is the New Going*

Jesus is alive . . . for real! And because he is alive for real, we can have a real discipleship relationship with our Savior. Those who read this book will find themselves encouraged to a deeper walk with Jesus that takes us beyond following Christ's example to seeking to be discipled by Jesus himself.

VINCENT BACOTE, author of *The Political Disciple*

The bar has been set much too low. We have settled for much too little. Jesus didn't call people to be "Christian" as the world defines that term. He calls people to follow him. I am excited about this book, which reminds us of this very fact: Jesus wants to disciple you.

BRIAN NYE, director, Legacy Disciple

So often we disciple the way that we've been discipled (if we were discipled), but we fail to reflect on whether or not we're discipling as Jesus would. As imperfect human beings, is it even possible to disciple as Jesus did? Or is there another way? In this book, Robert presents an alternative way forward, one where the role of the pastor is not to disciple people, but rather, to prepare them to be discipled by Jesus instead.

DANIEL IM, author of *No Silver Bullets: 5 Small Shifts that Will Transform Your Ministry*, coauthor of *Planting Missional Churches*, director of church multiplication at newchurches.com, and teaching pastor at The Fellowship, Nashville

DISCIPLED
by JESUS

—— + ——

*Your Ongoing Invitation
to Follow Christ*

N

W

E

S

ROBERT GELINAS

NAVPRESS

A NavPress resource published in alliance
with Tyndale House Publishers, Inc.

NavPress is the publishing ministry of The Navigators, an international Christian organization and leader in personal spiritual development. NavPress is committed to helping people grow spiritually and enjoy lives of meaning and hope through personal and group resources that are biblically rooted, culturally relevant, and highly practical.

For more information, visit www.NavPress.com.

Discipled by Jesus: Your Ongoing Invitation to Follow Christ

Copyright © 2018 by Robert Gelinas. All rights reserved.

A NavPress resource published in alliance with Tyndale House Publishers, Inc.

NAVPRESS and the NAVPRESS logo are registered trademarks of NavPress, The Navigators, Colorado Springs, CO. *TYNDALE* is a registered trademark of Tyndale House Publishers, Inc. Absence of ® in connection with marks of NavPress or other parties does not indicate an absence of registration of those marks.

The Team:
Don Pape, Publisher
David Zimmerman, Acquisitions Editor
Elizabeth Symm, Copy Editor
Libby Dykstra, Designer

Published in association with the literary agency of Wolgemuth & Associates, Inc.

Cover illustration of compass drawn by Libby Dykstra. Copyright © Tyndale House Publishers, Inc. All rights reserved.

Cover photograph of gold texture copyright © by Ruslan Zelensky/Creative Market. All rights reserved.

All Scripture quotations, unless otherwise indicated, are taken from the Holy Bible, *New International Version,*® *NIV.*® Copyright © 1973, 1978, 1984, 2011 by Biblica, Inc.® Used by permission. All rights reserved worldwide. Scripture quotations marked ESV are taken from *The Holy Bible*, English Standard Version® (ESV®), copyright © 2001 by Crossway, a publishing ministry of Good News Publishers. Used by permission. All rights reserved. Scripture quotations marked KJV are taken from the *Holy Bible*, King James Version. Scripture quotations marked NKJV are taken from the New King James Version,® copyright © 1982 by Thomas Nelson, Inc. Used by permission. All rights reserved.

Some of the anecdotal illustrations in this book are true to life and are included with the permission of the persons involved. All other illustrations are composites of real situations, and any resemblance to people living or dead is purely coincidental.

Every effort has been made to obtain permission from copyright holders to reproduce "So Send I You." Any queries relating to copyright in this content should be referred to NavPress for immediate attention.

For information about special discounts for bulk purchases, please contact Tyndale House Publishers at csresponse@tyndale.com, or call 1-800-323-9400.

Cataloging-in-Publication Data is available.

ISBN 978-1-63146-828-5

Printed in the United States of America

24	23	22	21	20	19	18
7	6	5	4	3	2	1

To Colorado Community Church.
Serving you as you wash the feet of our city
is among the great joys of my life.

CONTENTS

INTRODUCTION

The Coming Reformation in Discipleship

———— + ————

"Have you been discipled?"

That was a question I grew up with. I heard it frequently in the Christian circles I was a part of, along with its counterpart: "Are you discipling somebody?"

I didn't quite understand either of these questions. What did it actually mean to "be discipled" or to "disciple someone else"? Nevertheless, I assumed, based on the questions, that my spiritual growth was dependent on filling in blanks: "I was discipled by _____." "I am discipling _____."

Maybe the blank was "John," maybe "Su Lin," or maybe "my youth pastor." Whoever it was, no one told me that it might be *Jesus*.

This wasn't a malevolent omission. No one was hiding Jesus from me. Rather, they were simply passing on a well-meaning but incomplete view of what Jesus meant when he said, "Go and make disciples."

Jesus—as I will argue in this book—is still personally

discipling people today. This reality can be difficult for us to understand or accept, especially since Jesus ascended into heaven (Acts 1:9). We can be forgiven for thinking that discipleship is all up to us; however, before Jesus left, he made promises:

- He will be with us whenever we desire to connect with him (Matthew 18:20).
- He will be with us wherever we may find ourselves (Matthew 28:20).
- Jesus may not be immediately visible to us, but he is intimately present to all of us (John 17:22-23).

Jesus is ready, willing, and able to do for us what he did for the Twelve. And as we see with the original disciples, beautiful realities become possible when Jesus is discipling you. The early Christians stepped into a world in which women were owned, children were cheap labor, poverty was the lot of the majority, slavery was assumed, disabled people were discarded, religion was incarcerating, and government was oppressive. By the time Jesus' first disciples spilled their blood on the streets of Rome, they had turned their world upside down. They reintroduced love and covenant into marriage, providing a safe haven for women and children (Ephesians 5:25-33). There were no needy people among them because those who had much ensured that no one had too little (Acts 2:42-47; 4:32-37). Though the institution of slavery remained, it became obsolete as slave and owner worshiped the one true Master together (Galatians 3:26-29; Philemon 1:1-25). Those with disabilities were recognized as full-fledged bearers of God's image, counted worthy to suffer like Jesus (Genesis 1:26; 2 Corinthians 12:1-10). Believers permeated the government, even in Caesar's household (Philippians 4:22), and new names were written daily in the Book of Life.

Three years with Jesus prepared them for all of that!

Jesus desires to do the same with us. We can be a part of that revolutionary movement of Kingdom transformation, bringing bucketloads of people into a relationship with God. If we allow him, he can show us what it looks like to live transformative lives in our world of terrorism, mass incarceration, fatherlessness, oppression, an overflowing foster care system, and racial divides both inside and outside the church. Jesus can do with our lives in three years what no church can do in thirty—what no corporation or organization has done in centuries, what no government or religion has done in millennia.

I love what it says in the book of Acts about those original disciples. When people watching them "realized that they were unschooled, ordinary men, they were astonished and they took note that these men had been *with* Jesus" (Acts 4:13, italics added). There wasn't much to note about the first disciples. They were like you and me—typical folks. What *was* noteworthy was that they had spent time with Jesus himself. That's the way it was and is supposed to be. Christian community is essential, but when it comes to your discipleship, why would you settle for anyone else?

Off Course by a Few Degrees

There was a time in my life when I had to stop and ask, "What did Jesus actually mean when he said, 'Go and make disciples'?" (Matthew 28:19). I'd been a Christian for decades (a pastor too!), but I'd never learned the meaning of discipleship. I was on autopilot, just accepting what others said about discipleship but never discovering on my own. Oftentimes, the essentials of the Christian life can become so familiar and commonplace for us that we fail to see the obvious, let alone the nuances of our faith.

I've read dozens of books on discipleship. Attended conferences. Pored over the research. My investigation into the meaning of "go and make disciples" has led me to believe that many of us are missing out on what Jesus is actually offering us.

- We have an insufficient definition of discipleship—we can't know what a disciple is until we remember what a disciple was.
- Because the average Christian doesn't know what a disciple is, we don't really know how to lead others to become one.
- Despite deep desire for real-life transformation, most of our discipleship activities are falling short of our hopes.

What I've concluded is this: We need a reformation in discipleship.

During the sixteenth century, it became clear that when it came to how people enter into a relationship with God, we were missing the mark. The church was taking the place of Jesus in the salvation stories of his people. Then along came people like Martin Luther to remind us of what we already knew: namely, that we are saved by grace through faith alone in Christ alone. We remember this course correction as the Reformation.

Once again, the church has lost its way. Today, when it comes to discipleship, the church is sitting in the seat reserved for Jesus alone.

A ship off course by a few degrees at sea will end up at the wrong destination. Similarly, at the tee box, if a golfer's clubhead is slightly off at the moment of impact with the ball, the ball will wind up in the rough. In the short term, slight miscalculations don't matter so much. But as time passes and greater distance is traveled, the error becomes more pronounced.

When it comes to discipleship, the church has been slightly off course for a long time. "Making disciples" has become this thing we do to each other. We even made up a word: *discipleship*. You'll have a hard time finding this particular connotation of *discipleship* in the average dictionary because it's unique to us. It's the word we use to describe the things churches do in order to "make disciples." We are trying to do for others what Jesus ultimately desires to do himself.

This disciple-making development wasn't an intentional

miscalculation; as we'll discover, several factors made it difficult to stay on course. Nevertheless, somewhere along the way we took Jesus' place in people's discipleship, and we allowed other people to take Jesus' place in our discipleship.

How far off course are we? Today, average pastors assume it's their job to disciple people, and they in turn teach their congregation that they need to be discipled and that the programs and activities of the church are the means by which this should happen. Maybe you've had this experience: You began to attend a church—maybe you even became a formal church member—and then someone asked you to become part of a small group, or to engage in a midweek Bible study, or to meet one-on-one with somebody to work through a book together. There is nothing wrong with these activities, and as we'll see, they occupy an important place in the life of a believer. We need to know the Bible, learn how to share our faith, and understand the importance of generosity. But when their role is misunderstood, these activities become a wall around Jesus rather than a bridge to him.

We pastors sense that something is not working. We see that no matter how hard we try to get widespread participation in our "discipleship" programs, rarely is there full-fledged buy in. For those who do participate, the results are mixed. And if we're honest, we know that other forces in our culture (media and politics, for example) are more effective at influencing people's minds and behaviors. On our best days, we attempt to preach better sermons and strategize better approaches. On our worst days, we blame those sitting in our pews for not being fully committed.

We tell people that they need to be able to answer questions like "Who am I discipling?" and "Who is discipling me?" instead of asking together, "How is Jesus discipling me?" and "How is he discipling you?"

Goon Park and Van Gogh

During the 1930s, the psychology labs at the University of Wisconsin were affectionately nicknamed Goon Park. Housed at 600 N. Park Street, the lab's address when hastily scribbled looked like the word *goon*.[1] The moniker seemed to fit, however, for it was there that a young researcher by the name of Harry Harlow sought to prove a seemingly obvious thesis: Children need love from their mothers.

What seems like common sense to us was unconventional in Harlow's day. Prior to 1950, psychologists, doctors, and even the government believed differently. John B. Watson, the president of the American Psychological Association, stated, "When you are tempted to pet your child[,] remember that mother love is a dangerous instrument. . . . Once a child's character has been spoiled by bad handling, which can be done in a few days, who can say that the damage is ever repaired?"[2] In this era, it was even believed that "too much hugging and coddling could make infancy unhappy, adolescence a nightmare—even warp the child so much that he might grow up unfit for marriage."[3]

Warnings abounded in pamphlets with titles like "The

Dangers of Too Much Mother Love." Activities such as cuddling, kissing, and rocking a baby were considered bad parenting. Pediatricians warned that there were serious storms ahead for the over-kissed child. The guideline set for parents to follow? Don't kiss your child more than once a year![4]

In direct contradiction to the thinking of his day, Harlow believed that he could prove the importance of the mother-child bond. In one experiment, he constructed two artificial, surrogate mothers for infant rhesus monkeys. One was wiry, ugly, and cold, and provided milk to the infant monkeys. The other was warm and made of soft terry cloth, but provided no nourishment. A baby monkey was put in the cage with both "moms." What would the infant choose? Food or security? Sustenance or softness?

If the prevailing perspective of the day was correct, the infant monkey's choice was easy: It would bond with the "mother" that met its need for milk. That's not what the babies did, however. Videos of this experiment show Harlow explaining that the baby monkey spent minimal time with the cold mother, basically only the hour or so per day that was necessary for the infant to drink the milk it needed. On the other hand, the infant spent almost twenty hours a day with the warm, affectionate, cuddly mother that provided no food.

Harlow took his experiment further, turning the warm, cuddly mother into a "monster mother."[5] When the infant sought to cuddle, the fake mother monkey would shake violently until "the teeth and bones of the infant chattered in unison." Unbelievably, Harlow then added compressed air to blast the infant, brass spikes to poke it, and "an embedded steel frame that, on schedule or demand, would fling forward and hurl the infant monkey off the mother's body."[6] What happened? The baby returned continually to the comfort monkey despite the abuse she sometimes subjected the baby to.

The results were clear: Nourishment is a necessity—but so is affection. Children need more than the bare essentials from their mothers. Harlow demonstrated what we all now take as a given: A mother's love matters.

Unfortunately, Harlow ignored another obvious question: What's the value of a *father's* love? By all accounts, Harry Harlow wasn't a good dad. His four children from two different marriages mostly remember him as absent. He proved that a mother is more than a milk machine, but he failed to explore whether or not a father is more than a paycheck.

When it comes to discipleship, we, too, have failed to see the obvious. Many have sounded clarion calls declaring that we need better disciples. Conferences, books, and curricula highlight the importance of discipleship. Like Harry Harlow, we have sought to demonstrate the change that needs to happen. But along the way, we have made a mistake similar to his. We have overlooked an essential element to discipleship—Jesus.

In his beautiful book *The Divine Commodity: Discovering a Faith beyond Consumer Christianity*, Skye Jethani wrote about Vincent van Gogh's complicated relationship with Christianity. Van Gogh used the color yellow in his paintings to symbolize the presence of God. In works like *The Sower* and *Olive Trees*, the color is lavish and prominent. Yellow virtually fills the canvas in his depiction of *The Raising of Lazarus*. He takes a much subtler approach with *The Potato Eaters* as a very slight yellow haze of faith illuminates the darkness.

Van Gogh's struggle, Jethani wrote, "was primarily with the institutional church, not Christ. In his final years, as his mental illness became more severe, van Gogh reveals a profound devotion to Jesus while remaining disillusioned with the church."[7] Jethani draws our attention to *Starry Night*, a prominent painting from this period in Van Gogh's life, in which Van Gogh nestles a quiet countryside village beneath a swirling night-sky of brilliant blue and heavenly bodies in yellow. "The divine light of the stars is repeated in the village below, every home illuminated with the same yellow warmth. . . . But there is one building in van Gogh's imaginary village with no light, no divine presence—the church."[8]

I don't share Van Gogh's bleak view of church. While we may have flaws, I don't think we have locked God out. My experience is that most deeply desire God. However, I do see that in our eagerness to serve Jesus and make him known, we sometimes sideline him in the process. One way we do this is when we fail to see his ongoing, active presence in our spiritual growth. Too often we have missed out on the obvious truth that Jesus—because he is alive—is ready, willing, and able to do for us as he did for the original Twelve.

You and I can be discipled by Jesus.

CHAPTER ONE

TWO WORDS
That Will Change Your Life

Two words worth underlining in your Bible: *Jesus himself.*
Let them inspire hope for what is possible in your relationship with God. Zero in on them and let them spark the imagination of your soul.

> Now that same day two of them were going to a village called Emmaus, about seven miles from Jerusalem. They were talking with each other about everything that had happened. As they talked and discussed these things with each other, *Jesus himself* came up and walked along with them.
>
> LUKE 24:13-15, EMPHASIS ADDED

Passover had ended. Like many of their fellow Jews, these two travelers had come to Jerusalem for the feast. Now they were traveling home. But as momentous as each Passover was, this particular feast had been singularly disruptive. Why were these two travelers so interested in what happened to Jesus? Because they were his disciples. They were engaged in deep dialogue as they attempted to figure out what happened to Jesus. While they were in Jerusalem, he was arrested and executed, but now they had heard the incredible rumor that he was, in fact, no longer dead. They debated the possibilities and probabilities and wondered aloud, "What does this mean for our lives?"

Then it happened. *Jesus himself* began to walk with them.

They didn't, however, immediately know who had joined them. We're not sure why they didn't recognize him. Perhaps their eyes were fixated on the ground, or maybe the sun, low in the evening sky, impeded their vision. We are told that they were "kept from recognizing him," which might indicate that something supernatural was taking place (Luke 24:16).[1] What's clear is that *Jesus himself* was with them that day.

He walked with them. More than that, *Jesus himself* talked with them:

He asked them, "What are you discussing together as you walk along?"

They stood still, their faces downcast. One of them, named Cleopas, asked him, "Are you the only

one visiting Jerusalem who does not know the things
that have happened there in these days?"

"What things?" he asked.

LUKE 24:17-19

Jesus himself asked them questions, sparking conversation. And because they didn't know who he was, they began
sharing with Jesus what happened to Jesus! They explained
to him, "We pinned our hopes on this would-be Messiah.
Then the Romans crucified him. This morning, some of our
friends went to the tomb; they said he wasn't there, that it
was empty. We're just trying to piece all of this together."

Then *Jesus himself* gave them an opportunity to grow in
their faith: "He said to them, 'How foolish you are, and how
slow to believe all that the prophets have spoken! Did not the
Messiah have to suffer these things and then enter his glory?'"
(Luke 24:25-26). Such a brazen approach for a would-be
stranger. But this was Jesus; he knew them—personally—
and was inviting them to enlarge their view of what God
can and cannot do. They were witnesses to the fulfillment
of God's promises, but they were failing to connect the dots.

Then comes my favorite part, *Jesus himself* teaching them:
"Beginning with Moses and all the Prophets, he explained to
them what was said in all the Scriptures concerning himself"
(Luke 24:27). He led them in a Bible study! They didn't
have the New Testament (they were living it!), but the Old
Testament contained plenty to point them to the Messiah.
Jesus could have easily drawn a connection between the

Passover lamb and the Passover they celebrated just days before. If he had, perhaps he showed them that they had just seen the ultimate sacrifice that sets people free from bondage. Maybe he showed them where it says the Messiah would be betrayed for thirty pieces of silver or how none of the bones in his body would be broken.[2]

During this Bible study, he most likely spent significant time with them in the book of Isaiah: "He was pierced for our transgressions, he was crushed for our iniquities . . . by his wounds we are healed" (Isaiah 53:5). I wonder if he pointed out how Job pre-called his resurrection when he said,

> I know that my redeemer lives,
>   and that in the end he will stand on the earth.
> And after my skin has been destroyed,
>   yet in my flesh I will see God;
> I myself will see him
>   with my own eyes—I, and not another.
>   How my heart yearns within me!
>
> JOB 19:25-27

Let this sink in: Jesus walked with, talked to, and taught them *himself.*

Is *Jesus himself* available to do these kinds of things in your life? Is this experience of God reserved only for those on the pages of our Bibles? Is living vicariously through them the best we can hope for?

Twelve Lucky Ones?

These travelers on the road to Emmaus weren't the first to be discipled by Jesus himself, of course. Peter, Andrew, James, and John were at work when Jesus showed up and called them to be his disciples (Matthew 4:18-22). Jesus ate dinner with Matthew the tax collector in Matthew's own home (Matthew 9:9-13). In all, he personally invited twelve people from different backgrounds into a direct discipleship relationship with him. It was intimate, face-to-face, and one-on-one. Jesus joked with them and assigned nicknames (Matthew 16:18; Mark 3:17). He sent them out on assignments and debriefed them afterward—coaching them in the ways of the Kingdom (Luke 10:1-24). They heard him teach and asked him questions about the meaning of his parables (for example, see Matthew 13:36). The Twelve saw Jesus tired, lonely, struggling, and anguished. When Jesus was disappointed, they were close enough to see it on his face. They knew firsthand that his love was real as they received training, instruction, correction, purpose, and inspiration from him. They were discipled by *Jesus himself.*

We find ourselves envious of these first disciples. We think, *If I were discipled by Jesus himself, then things would be different. I would be bolder in my witness, clearer in my mission, and closer to God. Faith would be so much easier.* But you and I weren't meant to gaze longingly at their incredible fortune. They weren't the lucky few who just happened to be born at the right time and place in history. Quite the opposite—they were prototypes for you and me. Their experience with Jesus demonstrates what life is supposed to be like for all of us.

Sometime during the centuries between them and us, we lost sight of this beautiful reality. Our modern view of discipleship is deficient. We've busied ourselves with activities—many good and well-meaning—that, ultimately, are far less than what God had in mind for those who abide in his Son. It wasn't unreasonable for us to assume that what they had was special and that we have to settle for something less now that Jesus has ascended into heaven. After all, they existed at the same time in history and occupied the same geographic space as Jesus. Jesus was physically present with them. But Jesus promised his real presence to us, too. Jesus told us that he will never leave us and that he will be with us for all time (Matthew 28:20).

When we forget this, we give honor and respect to Jesus when it comes to our spiritual growth while at the same time seeing him as peripheral, unnecessary. Dietrich Bonhoeffer, in his classic treatise *The Cost of Discipleship*, wrote, "Christianity without the living Christ is inevitably Christianity without discipleship."[3] Bonhoeffer saw that discipleship was inextricably linked to the active involvement of the resurrected Jesus. As Bonhoeffer so eloquently wrote, "Discipleship without Jesus Christ is a way of our own choosing."[4] We must go back and reclaim a first-century view of what it means to be a disciple if we are going to experience what the twelve disciples, two fellow travelers on the road to Emmaus, and many others learned from *Jesus himself.*

Any definition of discipleship that does not recognize the real presence of Jesus misses the point. *Discipleship is a direct, one-on-one relationship in which we are led by, taught by, and loved by Jesus himself.*

Biblical discipleship requires face-to-face encounters with Jesus, and that, for us, requires a risen rabbi. Discipleship, then, is inseparable from the Resurrection. Unfortunately, too much of what we call discipleship could happen with or without the one who was crucified, died, was buried, and on the third day rose again.

Eyes to See

Luke Timothy Johnson's book *Living Jesus: Learning the Heart of the Gospel* opens with this sentence: "It makes a big difference whether we think someone is dead or alive."[5] He goes on to explain that if we think someone is dead, then we don't expect to have actual interaction with them. Our relationship with them is based upon who they were and what they've left behind—past tense. However, if they are alive, then we expect a current, present-tense relationship. "The most important question concerning Jesus, then," Johnson continues, "is simply this: Do we think he is dead or alive?" If we truly believe Jesus rose from the dead, "what we learn *about* him must therefore include what we continue to learn *from* him."[6]

Continuing to learn *from* Jesus: That should be our expectation and experience. Jesus is still with us. He is available right now to teach us the ways of the Kingdom in a way that we will experience the *living* nature of God's Word. Our hearts will burn inside, for our rabbi is near.

The reality is this: *Jesus himself* is walking and talking with us. *Jesus himself* is teaching us directly. However, the Emmaus road story does leave us with this question: Do we recognize that it's him?

> As they approached the village to which they were going, Jesus continued on as if he were going farther. But they urged him strongly, "Stay with us, for it is nearly evening; the day is almost over." So he went in to stay with them.
>
> When he was at the table with them, he took bread, gave thanks, broke it and began to give it to them. Then their eyes were opened and they recognized him, and he disappeared from their sight.
>
> LUKE 24:28-31

Jesus is available to us as he was to these first-century disciples. However, what we learn from them is that it is possible to have Jesus fully engaged in our spiritual growth and yet, for any number of reasons, not recognize him. Sometimes it takes a special moment when our eyes are opened to this reality.

There is much we need to unlearn about discipleship, for there are many myths and misconceptions. What's clear is that he is present even now in this very moment. As we continue, ask Jesus to reveal himself to you.

Jesus, you are near.

You are that fellow traveler

who has always been with me.

Father, help me to see your Son,

not just as the one

who died on the cross

but as the one

who rose from the dead

and is actively involved

in my life right now.

Spirit of the living God,

open my eyes.

Amen.

CHAPTER TWO

THE DISCIPLESHIP
Myth

I was raised by my grandmother. Some of my earliest memories are of her taking me to church. Even before I was in kindergarten, Grandma made sure I went to Sunday school. Every Sunday I'd put on my suit: dark-green pants and a light-green coat, with a clip-on tie to match. My coat was adorned with all the pins I earned by memorizing Bible verses and keeping perfect attendance. My grandmother would drive me to church, park in front, and send me in to learn about God while she waited in the car. At the end of class, even when it was cold and snowing, I would walk out to find the car parked in the same spot. I'd hop in, and we'd head for home. I write further about her in my book *The*

Mercy Prayer,[1] but suffice it to say, God's grace was an affront to her sense of fairness and justice.

One day my Sunday school teacher asked us what it meant to have a relationship with God. We all threw out our best answers, but apparently my response was not acceptable, because when class came to an end, I was asked to remain. My teacher proceeded to share with me the plan of salvation. I sat as she drew a diagram with God on one side of the chalkboard and me on the other with a wide chasm between us. She said that I couldn't get to God, so God came to me in Jesus and built a bridge with his cross so I could know him. She then asked me if I wanted to give my life to Jesus.

I didn't understand what this meant, but she was an authority figure in my life and I wanted to please her. So I said yes.

Next thing I knew, we were on our knees together and she led me in prayer. I confessed my sins (which at the age of nine didn't take long!), asked God to forgive me, and told him that my life was his.

When I opened my eyes, my teacher was smiling and tearful. I was happy because she was happy, but I didn't quite know what was happening. She took me by the hand out to my grandmother, who must have been wondering why I was late. My teacher exclaimed, "Little Robbie gave his life to Jesus!" and informed her that I needed to be in the worship service next week.

The following Sunday, I was in the first church service of my life. After the singing, praying, and preaching came the closing song, which was the beginning of the altar call. My

Sunday school teacher grabbed me by the hand, led me down front, and told the church, "Little Robbie gave his life to Jesus last week!" Everybody applauded. I was happy because they were happy, but I still didn't understand the implications of what was taking place.

Two weeks later, I was in the second worship service of my life, wearing a white robe and standing in water up to my neck. The pastor said, "I baptize you in the name of the Father, the Son, and the Holy Spirit."

As I fell backward into the water, it was as if time stopped. When you are a little boy who doesn't know who your daddy is, there are certain words you don't miss. "Father," the pastor had said. "I baptize you in the name of the Father . . ."

I was never the same. Best I can tell, I went in the water an orphan and came out a child of God. That was the beginning of me being fathered by God.

Soon thereafter, I asked my grandmother for a Bible. Guess I figured that if my Dad had written a book, I wanted to read it. Feeling a little intimidated and not knowing where to start reading, I decided on the book of James—it was short and felt manageable. In James, I discovered the kind of religion that makes God smile (James 1:27). I then decided to tackle the book of Revelation, which scared me so much that several months went by before I picked up the Bible again.

As confused and scared as I was, though, I couldn't stay away long. I was drawn to it because whenever I opened its pages, I heard the voice of my Father. Through the Scriptures, he affirmed me, corrected me, and taught me what it meant to be a man after his own heart. Jesus taught us to pray to "Our Father" for a reason. It's because God is literally available and desires to be "Our Daddy." When we surrender our hearts and lives to him, he makes up for the shortcomings, imperfections, or absences of our earthly fathers.

Shortly after my baptism, for reasons I still don't understand, I made another decision: I was going to start cussing. No longer would I censor my vocabulary. I was not going to deprive myself of all the words that my friends so freely partook. As far as I was concerned, I had missed out long enough. So late one night, I thought it through and made a plan. The anticipation alone kept me from sleeping much that night. When I arrived at school, I walked up to the first familiar face I saw and greeted him with a myriad of expletives. With a shocked look, he asked if I was okay—even a fellow student could tell this was out of character for me. It didn't feel as exhilarating as I had expected, but I continued nonetheless. At recess, I found a group of my friends standing together and eased into the circle. During a lull in the conversation, I proceeded to string together a series of words that would make any sailor proud. I walked away, leaving my friends and their baffled looks.

Then I felt it. It was a hand at my back, and then something more than that . . . a presence surrounding me. It was God my Father. He was so gentle. I didn't feel punished or even like he was disciplining me, more like he was redirecting me as his son. In his book *Fathered by God*, John Eldredge wrote,

You are the son [or daughter] of a kind, strong, and
engaged Father, a Father wise enough to guide you
in the Way, generous enough to provide for your
journey, offering to walk with you every step.

This is perhaps *the* hardest thing for us to
believe—really believe, down deep in our hearts,
so that it changes us forever, changes the way we
approach each day.[2]

That describes my experience. Throughout the course of
my life, I have lived fathered by God. Every step of the way
and in every season in my life, my experience of God as a
father has been tangible and real. Which brings me to my
point: If we can be fathered by God, we can also be discipled
by Jesus. Jesus actually tied these two concepts together when
he said,

You are not to be called "Rabbi," for you have one
Teacher, and you are all brothers. And do not call
anyone on earth "father," for you have one Father,
and he is in heaven. Nor are you to be called
instructors, for you have one Instructor, the Messiah.

MATTHEW 23:8-10

When Jesus says that we should "not call anyone on earth
'father,'" he's not literally saying that we are to withhold this
term of endearment from the men who raise us. Rather, he's
pointing out that a greater father is available to you and me.

The same is true when he says, "You are not to be called 'Rabbi'" and "Nor are you to be called instructors, for you have one Instructor, the Messiah." The point is identical: A greater teacher is available to you. Don't miss out on being discipled by Jesus.

Jesus Is Not a Model

The myth of modern-day discipleship is simply this: Jesus is the model we are to follow as we make disciples.

It sounds good and true. Who could argue with Jesus being our model for discipleship? After all, aren't we called to imitate Christ? What's wrong with saying that Jesus left us the example that we are to emulate as we disciple people? But to think of Jesus as our model is to subtly displace Jesus from the center of our spiritual growth. We pay homage to his ways of doing ministry, but we place other people (even ourselves) in the discipleship driver's seat.

When we say Jesus is our *model*, we become the central acting agent in discipleship. Jesus is relegated to Hall-of-Fame status for his past accomplishments. We are now the players on the field; his jersey has been retired, on display to inspire us each time we walk by.

By considering Jesus as merely a model for what we do, we miss that he is intimately involved in and in charge of the process. Jesus is not a paint-by-numbers template that we mimic. He is the artist whose paintbrushes are still in his hands. Jesus is so much more than a method to be mimicked.

This is why so many of us are drawn to the writings of

Dallas Willard. He was a discipleship reformer, a modern-day Martin Luther whose writings awakened us to what could be in our relationship with Jesus. Willard once noted that modern-day discipleship is not "recognizable as discipleship in terms of biblical teaching or of the Christian past."[3] Drawing upon the work of Jess Moody, he said that "churches are filled with 'undiscipled disciples.'"[4] His answer was not for the church to come up with programs to address the problem, however. Rather, he called us back to true discipleship with his vision of Christians being apprenticed by Jesus. "The eternal life, from which many profound and glorious effects flow, is *interactive relationship with God and with his special Son, Jesus, within the abiding ambience of the Holy Spirit.* . . . We learn to walk this way through apprenticeship to Jesus."[5]

Prepositions matter. We are disciples *of* Jesus, not *on behalf of* Jesus. We aren't to be discipled *in the way that* Jesus discipled. No, we are apprentices, each of us—students *of* Jesus himself.

Skye Jethani says that our misunderstanding of discipleship pertains to our posture toward God. Too many of us are living life from God, over God, for God, and under God, when the Bible gives us a better way: life *with* God. "God established a garden in Eden where he placed the man and woman and where he walked *with* them," Jethani writes. "God welcomed humanity into the eternal communion he had known since before time. We were created in his image so that we might live in relationship with him."[6] This vision of life with God wasn't just for Adam and Eve, for Jesus is Immanuel—God with us (Matthew 1:23). How we see Jesus sharing life with his disciples is how God shares his life with us.

In contrast, Kenneth Boa warns that "those who are active in discipleship ministries face the ever-present danger of supposing that the people they nurture are their disciples." Before we dismiss what he says as a matter of semantics, he notes, "When this happens, several negative consequences can follow."[7] A discipler must take on many roles in a fellow believer's life. For example, the discipler must be

- A mother who nurtures the newborn converts with love, protection, and nourishment.
- A father who sets boundaries for the young Christian through training and teaching.
- A coach who contributes to maturity and the growing independence of the disciple.
- A peer who meets the relational needs of the person in order to bring about a fruitful life.

"No single discipler," Boa concludes, "can effectively fill all these roles in the life of a disciple."[8] No one except Jesus. People are Jesus' disciples, not ours.

Perhaps you've heard it said that we all are to be "disciples who make disciples who make disciples," or that we all need to disciple people in relationships "like Jesus did." As well intentioned as statements like these are, we need to be careful with our language. Jesus has an important role for us to play in each other's spiritual growth, but it's Jesus—not us—at the center of people's discipleship.

I'm grateful for Dallas Willard. His vision of apprenticeship reminds us to keep "our eyes on Jesus, the pioneer and perfecter of [our] faith" (Hebrews 12:2). He reminds us that while discovering a biblical worldview, memorizing Scripture, learning how to share our faith, going to seminary, joining a vibrant small group or weekly prayer meeting, and attending a Bible-believing church are all good and valuable activities, we must not confuse them with actually being discipled by Jesus.

Jesus Was?

I was reading a book on discipleship when I encountered this sentence: "Jesus was the *master* disciple maker."[9] I underlined it because I absolutely agree. When it comes to making disciples, it doesn't get any better than Jesus. What he did with the original Twelve over the course of three years was astonishing. Where they started from and where they ended up was absolutely astounding.

The more I thought about this remarkable phrase, however, the more I realized that the sentence was incomplete. I took my pen and put a line through the word *was* and added the word *is*: Jesus *is* the *master* disciple maker!

Jesus is alive! As important as a church is, it cannot take the place of Jesus. Pastors are necessary, but they are no substitute for a direct discipleship relationship with Jesus. Jesus can do in three years what no church, pastor, small group, or book could do in a lifetime. The master disciple maker is available to disciple *you* himself.

Martin Luther King Jr. was raised in the church: His father was a pastor. From an early age, he was taught the story of Scripture. His brilliance was quickly evident, as he skipped two grades in high school and entered college at the age of fifteen. By the age of twenty-six, King had earned his PhD in theology and soon thereafter was called to pastor a church in Montgomery, Alabama. At the age of twenty-seven, he was asked to lead the local bus boycott there.

This was a trying and terrifying time in his life. One night, after receiving a threat-filled phone call, he experienced what has become known as his "Vision in the Kitchen." On many occasions, King recalled that

> something said to me, you can't call on daddy now;
> he's in Atlanta, a hundred-seventy-five miles away.
> . . . You've got to call on that something, on that
> person that your daddy used to tell you about, that
> power that can make a way out of no way. And I
> discovered then that religion had to become real to
> me and I had to know God for myself. And I bowed
> down over that cup of coffee. I never will forget it.
> Oh yes, I prayed a prayer. And I prayed out loud
> that night. I said, "Lord, I'm down here trying to do
> what's right. I think I'm right. I think the cause that
> we represent is right. But Lord, I must confess that

I'm weak now, I'm faltering, I'm losing my courage, and I can't let the people see me like this because if they see me weak and losing my courage they will begin to get weak.[10]

Jesus himself met Martin Luther King Jr. that night. He would later recount that he heard a voice say, "Martin Luther, stand up for righteousness. Stand up for justice. Stand up for truth. And lo, I will be with you, even until the end of the world." After that experience, he said, "I was ready to face anything."[11] When his house was bombed three days later, it is said that King was not visibly shaken. I believe that it was Jesus himself who prepared him for that experience.[12]

I also believe that Jesus is preparing you and me for the Kingdom moments that will come our way. In his sovereignty, he coordinates our past and present as he guides us toward the future. Jesus *is* the master disciple maker.

CHAPTER THREE

EMBRACING JESUS
as Your Pastor

It was one of the most terrifying moments of assurance that I've ever experienced.

When I was in college, there was this wonderful empty-nested couple who allowed me to live rent-free in their basement. A true blessing for a broke college student. One night, I awoke to someone calling my name. In the dark, I inquired back, "Yes?" But then I remembered that Bob and Juv were away on vacation. Who could it be?

I walked upstairs apprehensively, looking around and checking the front door and the driveway. No one. Puzzled and a bit unsettled, I returned to my bedroom.

As I began to settle into bed, once again, I heard a voice

calling my name. It was then that I recognized it—the same voice I had heard just a few years earlier.

As a high school freshman, I decided that I was going to be an orthopedic surgeon, primarily because I liked the idea of helping people while making a comfortable living. One day during cross-country practice, I took an awkward step and broke a bone in my left foot. *This is God at work in my life*, I thought. *Before I can be a doctor, I must first know what it's like to be a patient.* My physician said healing should take six weeks, but in reality, I was on crutches for six months. When the cast was finally removed, I was so happy that I (ill-advisedly) ran home from the hospital! I was back training shortly thereafter, but less than two months later, during warm-ups at track practice, I felt a snap. I had broken the same bone in the same place. The two X-rays looked virtually identical.

One evening, I propped my leg up with a pillow, hoping for some relief from the throbbing pain. Half-seated in my bed, I picked up my Bible and turned to Proverbs. I'll never forget what happened next. As I read, "Commit to the LORD whatever you do" (Proverbs 16:3), I was startled by a voice. It said, "I want you to be a pastor."

Fast-forward to Bob and Juv's dark basement, the same voice, this time calling my name, "Robert." I didn't know what to expect next. Was he, feet like brass and eyes like fire, about to appear in my room? Isaiah-like confession flooded my mind ("I am a man of unclean . . .") as I slid off my bed, facedown onto the carpet. Heart pounding within, I spoke out loud the first words that came to mind: "Speak, Lord, for your servant is listening."

I waited in the silence (I can still feel the carpet's texture on my lips), but that was it. I heard nothing else.

God was indeed working in and through the circumstances of my life, slowing me down enough so that my heart and soul could hear. That was the beginning of my trying to understand this humbling reality: Jesus calls us by name.

Jesus Our Pastor

Jesus' intentions are clear. He has declared the kind and quality of relationship he wants to have with you. Jesus wants to be your pastor.

> Very truly I tell you Pharisees, anyone who does
> not enter the sheep pen by the gate, but climbs in
> by some other way, is a thief and a robber. The one
> who enters by the gate is the shepherd of the sheep.
> The gatekeeper opens the gate for him, and the
> sheep listen to his voice. He calls his own sheep by
> name and leads them out. When he has brought
> out all his own, he goes on ahead of them, and his
> sheep follow him because they know his voice. But
> they will never follow a stranger; in fact, they will
> run away from him because they do not recognize
> a stranger's voice.
>
> JOHN 10:1-5

It's easy to lose sight of what Jesus is making available to us. In this passage, our Savior presents himself to us as a shepherd. This opens the door for a new way of seeing his activity in our lives: As the shepherd of our souls, he wants to personally tend, keep, guide, and direct us. He wants to lead us to flourishing fields where our spirits can graze and grow. He wants to pastor us himself.

Hardly a day goes by without someone calling me "Pastor." Yet for much of my adult life, I've had an ambivalent relationship with the title. When someone calls me "Pastor," I usually respond by saying, "Please, feel free to call me Robert." I love being a pastor, but the title has always felt like a suit tailor-made for someone else. To be discipled by Jesus is to recognize him as our pastor, that is, the one who shepherds our spiritual growth.

A shepherd sometimes leads his sheep by teaching them to follow the ringing of a bell. Once the flock has been trained to recognize the sound, he then puts the bell around the neck of one of his rams and keeps that particular sheep close to him. When the shepherd and this ram begin to walk, the bell rings and the other sheep follow. This is where we get our term *bellwether*. This imagery has helped me a lot. A pastor such as myself is simply a sheep with a bell around its neck. The Chief Shepherd himself continues to pastor us and the people who call us pastor.

Embracing Jesus in this way does not devalue the God-given role of local church pastors; rather, it changes what we expect from them. Scripture is clear: God gave pastors "to equip his people for works of service, so that the body of Christ may be built up until we all reach unity in the faith and in the knowledge of the Son of God and become mature, attaining to the whole measure of the fullness of Christ" (Ephesians 4:12-13). According to Paul, a pastor's role is twofold: point people to Jesus and mobilize them for service.

Pastors spend their time identifying the needs of their community and preparing God's people to meet those needs for the glory of God and the good of the city. In addition to that, their preaching, teaching, and leadership point people to a risen Savior, so that God's people have a unified experience of Jesus—"attaining to the whole measure of the fullness of Christ." My job as a pastor is not to disciple people but to prepare them to be discipled directly by Jesus, their Great Shepherd, and then equip the discipled. As the pastor of a local church, I should serve in such a way that people catch a compelling glimpse of all that is available to them in Christ while at the same time being careful not to take his place in their lives. We pastors must do what we do in such a way that people move to the edge of their seats in eager anticipation of Jesus himself stepping into their lives and guiding them directly.

One time, a man made an appointment to meet with his pastor. As he shared about a difficult decision he had to make, he expected his pastor to give him advice and perhaps some Scriptures for guidance. He was surprised when his pastor said, "I don't know the answers to the questions you are asking. These kinds of things are not specifically addressed in the Bible. But we know Jesus is here and loves you. So let's ask him." His pastor then dimmed the lights, turned some music on in the background, and said, "Let's ask Jesus together." The man prayed, asking Jesus for guidance as his pastor knelt before him in silent prayer. They prayed and waited for almost an hour. Then—suddenly—the man's eyes began to well up with tears. Jesus, his true pastor, by his Spirit began to reveal to him what he desired.

Seeing Jesus as our pastor gives us a helpful starting point as to what it actually looks like to be directly discipled by him. It all begins with him calling us by name. As Jesus said, his sheep listen because "he calls his own sheep by name" (John 10:3). Even though you are one of more than seven billion people on this planet, Jesus could spot you in the crowded corridors of a sports stadium or see you across the room at a party, walk up to you, and call you by name. When Jesus walked the earth, this was an ordinary occurrence. Looking up and seeing Zacchaeus in the tree, he called him by name (Luke 19:1-6). Jesus' first word to Saul as he confronted him on the road to Damascus was his name (Acts 9:1-5). Jesus, our Shepherd, calls us by name.

In John 10, Jesus invites us to imagine two shepherds who have commingled their flocks for the night. When morning comes, they have no problem separating the sheep into their respective groups because each sheep knows the voice of its shepherd. "They will never follow a stranger; in fact, they will run away from him because they do not recognize a stranger's voice" (John 10:5). They—small brains and all—recognize with distinct clarity his voice as he intimately calls them by name.

To be discipled by Jesus is to have your true pastor call you by name. You are not a generic, unidentifiable face in the midst of an amorphous blob of crowded humanity. No, God sees you and me and knows our true identity. As God declared through the prophet Isaiah, "This is what the LORD says—he who created you, Jacob, he who formed you, Israel: 'Do not fear, for I have redeemed you; I have summoned you by name; you are mine'" (Isaiah 43:1).

Jesus even had nicknames for his original flock. The moniker he gave James and John was *Boanerges*—Sons of Thunder—for apparently, they had a way of making their presence known (Mark 3:17). "Rocky" was his pet name for Peter (Matthew 16:18), though to make a point he reverted back to calling Peter by his given name, Simon (John 21:15-17). Or remember Mary recognizing Jesus when he called her by name (John 20:11-18)?

Jesus, your pastor, also knows your name and promises new names for eternity: "I will also give that person a white stone with a new name written on it, known only to the one who receives it" (Revelation 2:17).

This is not to say that each of us will have a moment when we hear an audible voice calling our name. In fact, many people of great faith, admirable followers of Jesus, would say they've never heard God speak audibly. That being said, please be open to the possibility of Jesus speaking directly to you.

My experience is that he is already speaking—through his Word, circumstances, other people, and, yes, his still, small voice—but we struggle to hear him, for we have neglected practices that create the space needed for us to listen.

When he was young, the Old Testament prophet Samuel had a hard time discerning the voice of God. The Lord called Samuel's name, but the boy thought it was the high priest, Eli, calling. Each time he heard the voice, Samuel mistakenly went to Eli, for we are told, "Samuel did not yet know the LORD: The word of the LORD had not yet been revealed to him" (1 Samuel 3:7).

> A third time the LORD called, "Samuel!" And Samuel got up and went to Eli and said, "Here I am; you called me."
>
> Then Eli realized that the LORD was calling the boy. So Eli told Samuel, "Go and lie down, and if he calls you, say, 'Speak, LORD, for your servant is listening.'" So Samuel went and lay down in his place.
>
> The LORD came and stood there, calling as at the other times, "Samuel! Samuel!"
>
> Then Samuel said, "Speak, for your servant is listening."
>
> 1 SAMUEL 3:8-10

If Eli had not been there, it might have been years before Samuel developed his ear and quieted his soul enough to recognize the voice of God. We need those who have the "ministry of Eli" in our lives, mentors who have walked the road we are now on and can help us recognize and hear our pastor's voice.[1]

To be called by name has to do with identity—a life defined first and foremost by Jesus alone. This brings us to the core of looking to Jesus as your pastor: love.

Our identity comes from allowing ourselves to be loved by Jesus. Jesus is the Shepherd who loves us so much that he leaves behind ninety-nine sheep so he can find us when we have wandered off. When he finds a lost sheep, "he joyfully puts it on his shoulders and goes home. Then he calls his friends and neighbors together and says, 'Rejoice with me; I have found my lost sheep'" (Luke 15:5-6). Your identity will forever change when you see yourself as the one whom Jesus carries joyfully on his shoulders. Our identity is solidified when we surrender to the truth that *God loves us and there's nothing we can do about it!*

This is truly good news for those of us who have been spiritually abused by a pastor. Too many have sat under teaching that resulted in condemnation, shame, and blame. Too many a pastor has sought to motivate through guilt and fear instead of the lavish love of God. A Jewish believer hearing Jesus describe himself as the Good Shepherd would have immediately thought of Ezekiel 34. In that passage, God laments that his people had to endure leaders who were fleecing them for ill-gotten gain, ruling harshly, and not lovingly searching for the lost nor nursing their wounds. Therefore, God promised,

I myself will search for my sheep and look after
them. As a shepherd looks after his scattered flock
when he is with them, so will I look after my sheep.
I will rescue them from all the places where they
were scattered. . . . I will tend them in a good pasture
. . . I myself will tend my sheep . . . I will search for
the lost and bring back the strays. I will bind up the
injured and strengthen the weak. . . . I will shepherd
the flock with justice.

EZEKIEL 34:11-12, 14-16

God's love is relentless, and we find comfort when we
"know that the LORD is God. It is he who made us, and we are
his; we are his people, the sheep of his pasture" (Psalm 100:3).

The call of our Shepherd comes with a new identity. This
was true even before Jesus was Jesus. In the Old Testament,
there is a mysterious figure known as "the angel of the Lord."[2]
Not to be confused with "an" angel of the Lord, "the" angel of
the Lord is seen as equal with God, speaks as God, redeems,
forgives, and even accepts worship. Interestingly, this mysterious one doesn't appear in Scripture after the manger, for,
I believe, the angel of the Lord was none other than the
preincarnate Christ.[3]

The first recorded appearance of the angel of the Lord was
to a young, scared single mother by the name of Hagar. She
was the mistreated slave of Abram and Sarai who ran away
from their household out of desperation. She was hungry,
alone, and with no way to provide for her baby when the

angel of the Lord appeared and called her by name: "Hagar, slave of Sarai, where have you come from, and where are you going?" (Genesis 16:8). She explained her predicament, and then the angel let her know that she and her child matter to God and his plans. He then provided direction for her life, for that is what the Good Shepherd does.

The angel of the Lord also appeared to Jacob, a man whose name literally meant "deceiver." That would be like naming your child "Little Liar"! Imagine how that name shaped Jacob's psyche. As he grew up, Little Liar swindled his brother out of his birthright and tricked his father out of the family blessing (Genesis 25:19-34; 27:1-45). Then one night, Jacob met the angel of the Lord. They wrestled until dawn, and then Jacob realized that this angel was more than an angel: "Your name will no longer be Jacob, but Israel, because you have struggled with God and with humans and have overcome" (Genesis 32:28).

That's powerful. And just in case Jacob didn't understand that this was to be a permanent name change, God confirmed it a few chapters later, saying, "Your name is Jacob, but you will no longer be called Jacob; your name will be Israel" (Genesis 35:10). Little Liar became "One with Whom God Wrestled."[4] For the rest of his life, he would be defined by his encounter with the angel of the Lord—Jesus.

What are the names you call yourself? Ex-con or Felon? Easy or Slut? Fatso, Lazy, or Stupid? Beware! Jesus is willing to take you to the mat so he can change your name.

In addition to an identity change, our shepherd calls us

for another reason: "He calls his own sheep by name and leads them out" (John 10:3). Jesus calls you because he is taking you somewhere. There is a destination—green pastures and quiet waters—that he has for you.

Direct Leading of Your Life

If Jesus is calling us, he's also leading us.

Shepherds lead and sheep follow. Jesus said, "When he has brought out all his own, he goes on ahead of them, and his sheep follow him because they know his voice" (John 10:4). Jesus takes the lead, and we stay as close as possible.

"Follow me." It was Christ's call to the twelve disciples.

Matthew sat in his tax-collecting booth when Jesus called, "*Follow me*" (Mark 2:14). Matthew's response was to stop what he was doing and follow his Shepherd.

Jesus encountered Philip on his way to Galilee and said, "*Follow me*" (John 1:43). Philip followed.

Peter was out fishing when Jesus shouted, "*Come, follow me . . . and I will send you out to fish for people*" (Matthew 4:19). Peter immediately dropped his nets and followed Jesus. After Peter's denial of Jesus, his Shepherd found him and renewed the call: "*Follow me*" (John 21:19, 22).

When the shepherd calls, the sheep follow.

The call of discipleship wasn't reserved for the Twelve. Jesus repeated it often:

- "Follow me, and let the dead bury their own dead" (Matthew 8:22).

- "Whoever wants to be my disciple must deny themselves and take up their cross and follow me" (Matthew 16:24).
- "Sell your possessions and give to the poor, and you will have treasure in heaven. Then come, follow me" (Matthew 19:21).
- "My sheep listen to my voice; I know them, and they follow me" (John 10:27).

"Follow me," the call to the Twelve, the call to the crowds, and also Jesus' call on our lives. But what does it mean to actually follow Jesus? Especially for us—two millennia removed from Christ's time on earth?

The standard answer goes like this: Once you give your life to Christ and are in a relationship with him, the goal is to understand what he did and then imitate his way of life as closely as you can. So to follow Jesus means that you read your Bible, with special attention to the Gospels, and take note of Jesus' life and teachings. And then do what he said.

This is a good start, but there is so much more. Yes, it's imperative that we know what Jesus did and said, but if we're going to be discipled by Jesus, we need to transition our language into the present tense. When we have reduced following Jesus to doing what he *did*, we have slipped back into a past-tense view of discipleship. Spiritual growth happens as we recognize that we can *still* follow Jesus the way first-century disciples did. *Following Jesus isn't just doing what he said; it's doing what he is saying.*

Jesus is still alive. Jesus is still speaking, and he is still calling you by name. He didn't say all he had to say in the first century. Therefore, to follow Jesus is to listen to what Jesus is saying to you right now. Trust me, he's talking to *you*.

To be discipled by Jesus is to be called by Jesus. To be called by Jesus, then, means we are being *led* (present tense) by Jesus. "He calls his own sheep by name and leads them out" (John 10:3).

The original Twelve experienced Jesus daily in the present tense. He hung out with them in normal, everyday life, teaching, guiding—shepherding. Even after Jesus rose from the dead and ascended to his Father, we see him continuing to lead them directly.

The Black Angel

Just north of downtown Denver, you'll find an overgrown, abandoned cemetery known as Riverside Cemetery tucked away. That is where Clara Brown, "the black angel of Gilpin," is buried. Born into slavery in Virginia in the early 1800s, Clara fell in love twice at the age of eighteen—first with Jesus and then with Richard, a fellow slave, who would become her husband. At the age of thirty-five, her owner died and her family was broken apart as the estate was liquidated. Clara was sold to George Brown in Kentucky. Over the next twenty years, she raised her new master's children while wondering about the fate of her own.

At the age of fifty-six, she gained her freedom and began searching for her family. She headed west, working as a domestic for those caught up in the gold rush, and eventually she ended up in Denver. She is thought to be Colorado's first black woman. Entrepreneurial in spirit, she moved to the mountains to work as a cook and midwife and started the first laundry service in the area. Amazingly, she saved thousands of dollars, bought sixteen lots of land in Denver, seven houses in Central City, and a few mines, as well. Despite being taken advantage of in a system that afforded her no justice and some fires and struggles along the way, she was able to amass a fortune.

More amazing than her earning was her giving. Methodist, Presbyterian, and Catholic churches were established in part due to her substantial gifts. She helped countless new settlers regardless of their race—black, white, and native people were the recipients of her affection.

In 1880, she moved back to Denver, as it was becoming too difficult for her to spend the winters in the high altitude of the mountains. She arrived with virtually nothing, for, it appears, she had given it all away. She had bankrupted her assets helping former slaves travel to Colorado, find work, start businesses, and get homes. She also sent many young women to college on scholarship. Through these events, she never stopped looking for her family. Year after year she wrote letters in search of her loved ones. She discovered that her husband, Richard, and her daughter, Margaret, had both died. There was no trace of her son, Richard Jr. Even so, Clara still hoped to find her other daughter, and in 1882, she received news that Eliza was alive.

In 1884, an anonymous gift allowed Clara to travel to Iowa, where she was united with her daughter and granddaughter. A year later, she died. Such an amazing story. Such a remarkable life. Upon her death, she was even honored in Colorado's capitol building.

To what did Clara attribute her ability to survive slavery, make money, and bless others lavishly? She said, "I always go where Jesus calls me."[5]

Jesus was her pastor. He called. She followed.

When encountering an unbeliever, we Christians have been known to ask, "Would you like to know how to have a personal relationship with Jesus?" It's a question designed to break through religion and get to the heart of the matter. Many times, people will answer questions about faith with replies like "I go to church" or "My grandfather was a pastor." But when we ask, "Do you have a personal relationship with Jesus?" we are stripping away all of the extraneous factors to get to the core of what we believe is possible. We want non-Christians to know that it's possible for them to have a personal relationship with the God of the universe.

Should we Christians start asking ourselves the same question? Perhaps we churchgoers and Bible readers need to ask the person looking back in our mirrors, "What about you? Do *you* have a personal relationship with Jesus?"

Is he your Shepherd?

Is he your pastor?

Is he your discipler?

Is he the one who calls you by name? Do you know his voice?

Is he the one who is leading you? Are you going where Jesus calls you?

To be discipled by Jesus is to know him like that.

CHAPTER FOUR

CHOOSING JESUS
as Your Teacher

Mary Magdalene woke up early Sunday morning and made her way to the tomb. Finding it empty, she asked the angels what they had done with Jesus. Turning around with tears in her eyes, she mistook Jesus for the gardener, but as soon as he called her by name, she recognized him. Then she exclaimed, "Rabboni!" (John 20:1-16).

The first word out of her mouth was not "Savior" or "Lord" or even "Rabbi" (teacher), but "Rabboni" ("*my* teacher"). The first thing that crossed her mind when she discovered Jesus was alive was that he was still available to be her rabbi, that she could still be discipled by Jesus.

Have you, like Mary, chosen Jesus as your primary

teacher? The résumé of this rabbi is remarkable. His credentials are impeccable.

- Not only does he understand photosynthesis, but he is also the Light of the World (John 1:4; 8:12).
- If you're interested in medicine, then you'll be happy to know that he is the Great Physician (Mark 2:17).
- If you are interested in engineering and architecture, then take note that he designed and built a church that has stood the test of time, and on top of that, he's gone away to prepare a place for you (Matthew 16:18; John 14:1-4).
- If you are interested in mathematics, then you're going to be amazed at what he can do with a few fish and loaves (John 6:1-15).
- If you are interested in finance, then Jesus can show you where to get an eternal return on your investment (Matthew 6:19-24; 25:14-30).
- As the King of kings, he can teach you anything you want to know about politics (Revelation 19:16).

Rabboni. The first title given to Jesus after he rose from the dead!

The Frog in Science Class

God's Word is meant to fill our minds, flow from our lips, and find a home in our hearts. When we engage the Scriptures in study and meditation, something happens, because God's word is alive—literally! God breathed the "breath of life" into

Scripture in the same way he did to Adam, Eve, and all living creatures (Genesis 1:30; 2:7; 2 Timothy 3:16-17).

There is a way to handle God's Word that treats it like a textbook, just a dry system of facts that we study so we can pass an exam. But the Bible is so much more than a book of information; it's a book that brings about transformation. In the Scriptures, we interact with the living God. I love what the Bible says about the Bible.

> The law of the LORD is perfect,
>> refreshing the soul.
> The statutes of the LORD are trustworthy,
>> making wise the simple.
> The precepts of the LORD are right,
>> giving joy to the heart.
> The commands of the LORD are radiant,
>> giving light to the eyes.
> The fear of the LORD is pure,
>> enduring forever.
> The decrees of the LORD are firm,
>> and all of them are righteous.
> They are more precious than gold,
>> than much pure gold;
> they are sweeter than honey,
>> than honey from the honeycomb.
> By them your servant is warned;
>> in keeping them there is great reward.

PSALM 19:7-11

God's Word has a purpose that cannot be thwarted. God insures that his Word accomplishes his predetermined intentions.

> As the rain and the snow
>> come down from heaven,
> and do not return to it
>> without watering the earth
> and making it bud and flourish,
>> so that it yields seed for the sower and bread
>>> for the eater,
> so is my word that goes out from my mouth:
>> It will not return to me empty,
> but will accomplish what I desire
>> and achieve the purpose for which I sent it.
>
> ISAIAH 55:10-11

God's Word is alive (Hebrews 4:12-13). As with any living organism, it needs to be handled with care. Remember what happened to the frog in high school science class? It entered the room croaking and jumping, full of life. But then we decided to study it. Pinned down on a board and cut open. We learned what its heart and liver looked like. Things once hidden were now in plain sight. In the process, however, something important was lost—the frog's life!

In the same way, we must be careful when we study the *living* Word of God. The Scriptures are a mystery revealed, a song sung, a way of life presented. They are meant to be pursued and experienced. They are more than a science project.

The Pharisees and teachers of the Law had a way of removing the living beauty from God's Word. In their hands, it was dry and dead. They dissected the intricacies of the Scriptures in a way that killed it for the sake of their own debating points. In contrast, life flowed through Jesus' teaching. He handled the Word differently than everybody else.

We see this dissecting approach when an expert in the Law attempted to test Jesus by asking, "What must I do to inherit eternal life?" (Luke 10:25-37). It's such an odd question because you don't earn an inheritance, you *receive* it. Jesus replied, "What is written in the Law? How do you read it?"

The teacher of the Law answered by quoting the ancient Shema: "Love the LORD your God with all your heart and with all your soul and with all your strength" (Deuteronomy 6:5). Jesus affirmed that he had answered well, but the teacher of the Law couldn't help himself. He continued to dissect God's Word by asking, "And who is my neighbor?"

Jesus, in turn, launched into a story about a dangerous road and a man attacked, robbed, and left for dead on the side of the road. Jesus' parable of the Good Samaritan resuscitated the discussion. He didn't dodge the question, but he answered it in such a way that treated the Word as a living species, infiltrating our "soul and spirit, joints and marrow," for the living Word of God "judges the thoughts and attitudes of the heart" (Hebrews 4:12).

As somebody who spends a large part of my time either preparing to teach or teaching, Jesus amazes me. I'm enthralled with his teaching. Every time I study him, I'm convinced that he was simply the greatest teacher who has ever walked this planet, the most brilliant teacher you could ever encounter.

When he taught, his listeners often didn't realize they were being taught. His material came from real life as he spoke about farmers and soil. He recognized the gritty reality of strained relationships, whether they were between a parent and child, a citizen and a government, or an ethnic group that you harbored prejudice against. With Rabbi Jesus, class was always in session as he developed analogies-on-the-go about birds, seeds, fruit trees, and lost things. His language transitioned seamlessly between the formal setting of the synagogue and gritty reality of the streets. He made you feel as essential as salt and as important as light. Outside the classroom your mind continued to ponder what he said as you kneaded yeast into a lump of dough and baked bread for your family.

Jesus wrapped truth in parables. This meant that if you wanted to understand the depth of his teaching, you would have to gnaw on his words like a dog trying to reach the marrow of its bone. Teaching this way, Jesus revealed the heart of those listening. If you weren't open to the things of God, then you could just dismiss his stories as interesting but ultimately meaningless. But if your heart wanted the things of God, then you would dive into the parable and find the truth, and upon discovering that truth, you could respond, "I must repent, for the Kingdom of Heaven is near!" The beauty of a parable is that once you understand the profound Kingdom truth within, you can turn around and explain the Kingdom of God to your friends in the same way Jesus communicated it to you.

As a teacher, Jesus was absolutely and utterly amazing! He was a jazz theologian constantly improvising on old standards, making them sound fresh and new. Like the other rabbis, Jesus taught from a seated position, but when he sat down, your heart, mind, and soul stood at attention . . . for he was a remarkable teacher (Matthew 5:1-2; Luke 4:20).

Now consider this. The same one who amazed the crowds—the greatest teacher to have ever lived—is available to teach you, too.

A Better Mousetrap

The Sermon on the Mount was Jesus' stump speech.[1] It comprises his core set of teachings. He would share these teachings when he was in a new place or before a new audience.[2] A crowd would form, and he would preach a variation of this message, covering a myriad of topics: from happiness and anxiety to prayer and fasting. He pulled no punches, either, taking on tough subjects such as sin, money, and eternity.

Jesus was fond of ending this message with a story about two men and their home-construction projects. One of the men foolishly built his house on topsoil; the other took his time and wisely dug down to bedrock to lay his foundation.

This metaphor caused Jesus' listeners to contemplate their own life choices and to rethink why some people stand strong through the difficulties of life while others do not. His point was clear. Storms are an inevitable part of life; therefore, we must take the time and build well today or we will pay the price tomorrow. We can blaze our own trail and do what seems expedient. Or we can heed his words and stand strong.

I envision Jesus delivering this message like a father telling the story of "The Three Little Pigs" to his toddler. With animated arms, he acts out falling rain, rising waters, and unrelenting wind. "Crash!" The house on the shallow foundation doesn't make it through the onslaught. Jesus wanted people contemplating discipleship to know that following him wouldn't be easy. Life with Jesus requires a willingness to dig deep.

This sermon had a profound effect on those who heard it. There was something about the way Jesus preached. When he spoke you felt understood, loved, and respected. Matthew, who records the most complete version of this message, tells us that people were deeply moved by what he had to say: "When Jesus had finished saying these things, the crowds were amazed at his teaching, because he taught as one who had authority, and not as their teachers of the law" (Matthew 7:28-29).

There was something striking about Jesus' teaching. It wasn't just what he said but how he said it. There's an old adage, often attributed to Ralph Waldo Emerson, that says, "If you write a better book, or preach a better sermon, or build a better mousetrap than your neighbor, though you build your house in the woods, the world will make a beaten path to your door." Jesus was preaching a better sermon, and the crowds flocked to hear what he had to say.

But notice what was better about the teaching of Jesus. The people didn't comment on how he structured his message or his use of humor. Nor did they point out his charisma or eloquent use of language. What amazed them was that "he taught as one who had authority."

Jesus had clout. As the Son of God, he possesses "all authority" (Matthew 28:18). Even powerful Roman soldiers recognized this (Luke 7:1-10). Jesus had what theologians call "intrinsic authority"—the sort of authority that comes not from a title or a diploma but by virtue of who you are. As John pointed out, Jesus is the very Word of God (John 1:1). Jesus spoke with a weightiness that was startling in comparison to what the crowds were used to. His gravitas was stark in comparison to the teachers of the Law, who focused on the external rather than the internal. They spent most of their time telling you what you had to do instead of inspiring your heart to want the ways of God. Jesus had harsh words for these kinds of teachers.

> Woe to you, teachers of the law and Pharisees, you hypocrites! You shut the door of the kingdom of heaven in people's faces. You yourselves do not enter, nor will you let those enter who are trying to.
> Woe to you, teachers of the law and Pharisees, you hypocrites! You travel over land and sea to win

a single convert, and when you have succeeded, you
make them twice as much a child of hell as you are.

MATTHEW 23:13-15

Strong words. Jesus called these leaders "blind guides" and
"snakes" because they loved the prestige of their position
more than they loved people (Matthew 23:16, 33). In comparison, the teaching of Jesus astounded the crowds and left
them flabbergasted.

Maybe you can relate. Have you ever wondered if you
really matter to the pastor preaching the sermon? Or have
you heard someone spend most of their time talking about
what the Bible does *not* say while never getting to what the
Bible actually *does* say? Or maybe you've read a book where
the author seemed more concerned about how everybody
else has the wrong interpretation of Scripture and how they
happen to be the only one with the right view? If so, then the
teaching of Jesus will amaze you, too.

We all need to be careful when we talk about the Christian
life. Sometimes we can make it sound so formulaic: A plus
B equals C. Just do these things and God will give you that
house, that spouse, that job of your dreams. These spiritual
formulas rarely add up and usually leave people wondering if
something is wrong with them—or, even worse, if something
is wrong with God's Word.

The teachers of the Law were rich in formulas and head
knowledge, but they didn't have the heart of God. That is
why Jesus warned us,

The teachers of the law and the Pharisees sit in
Moses' seat. So you must be careful to do everything
they tell you. But do not do what they do, for they
do not practice what they preach. They tie up heavy,
cumbersome loads and put them on other people's
shoulders, but they themselves are not willing to lift
a finger to move them.

MATTHEW 23:2-4

The teachers of the Law took those who wanted to know
God and made them feel inadequate and insignificant. They
held themselves up as the standard and handed out citations
for others' spiritual violations. They made God and his Word
feel far off and out of reach.

Then came Jesus.

Seven Demons

So now it should make even more sense why Mary, upon
encountering her resurrected Savior, greeted him with
"Rabboni"—my rabbi. She was at the tomb early that morning to honor the man who changed her life in an indescribable
way. And not only by his teaching. It was Jesus who set her
free from seven evil spirits.

Jesus traveled about from one town and village to
another, proclaiming the good news of the kingdom
of God. The Twelve were with him, and also some
women who had been cured of evil spirits and

diseases: Mary (called Magdalene) from whom seven demons had come out . . . and many others. These women were helping to support them out of their own means.

LUKE 8:1-3

Seven demons! Mary's life was a living hell—literally. But everything changed when she met Jesus because he had the authority to deal with that which tormented her. Fallen angels were no match for the one who created them. They had no choice but to obey his command to leave. Mary, indebted and grateful, dedicated herself and her resources to helping her deliverer set others free. She became a permanent part of Jesus' support team.

Mark emphasized her deliverance in his account of the Resurrection: "When Jesus rose early on the first day of the week, he appeared first to Mary Magdalene, out of whom he had driven seven demons" (Mark 16:9). Given this backstory, one would have expected her first words to Jesus to have been different. Knowing that Jesus cast seven demons out of her and saved her from a lifetime of suffering, what would you have expected her to say to Jesus when they met?

"My Redeemer"?

"My Deliverer"?

"My Savior"?

Yet, when she arrived at the empty tomb and came face-to-face with her risen Lord: "Woman, why are you crying? Who is it you are looking for? . . . Mary."

Her response: "Rabboni!"—my teacher (John 20:15-16).

As a student of Jesus' teaching and a beneficiary of his miracle-making power, Mary followed him wherever he went. She witnessed the remarkable nature of Jesus' teaching as he spoke to the crowds. The authority that Jesus exercised over her demons may have been a onetime occurrence in her life, but if Jesus was alive, then she could continue to experience his authority daily through his teaching.

What was true for Mary is true for us. If Jesus is alive, then you and I can be taught directly by the greatest teacher who has ever existed. To be discipled by Jesus means that the most awe-inspiring communicator is available to teach us, causing his Word to live and resuscitate our souls.

When that couple on the road to Emmaus reflected upon having Jesus as their own personal Sunday school teacher, they exclaimed, "Were not our hearts burning within us while he talked with us on the road and opened the Scriptures to us?" (Luke 24:32). This is to be our experience.

A man once asked me, "Do you really believe what you're saying? If Jesus, the greatest teacher ever, is available to teach all of us—Pastor, do you know what that means? We don't need you!" Exactly! God brings people into our lives to point us to Christ, but they are never to take the place of Christ. Jesus is the ultimate in every area of life. We human beings are signposts and shadows for each other at best. What Mary discovered is that once Jesus is your teacher, he's your teacher for life.

Once Your Teacher, Always Your Teacher

I can't do long division. I distinctly remember my teacher explaining it in elementary school. She diagrammed a long division problem on the board and walked us through each of the steps. She then assigned practice sheets for homework. That night I struggled to remember what to do and gave up in discouragement. The next day she went over the assignment with the class and asked, "Are there any questions? Does everybody understand?" I was too embarrassed to raise my hand, so I remained silent and was never asked the question again. It amazes me that I graduated from high school and earned bachelor's and master's degrees without ever having to demonstrate proficiency in this area. Thank God for calculators!

This sort of thing doesn't happen when Jesus is your teacher. Because Jesus is our rabbi for life, he takes the time to make sure we understand all of his Kingdom curriculum. He even understands the unique learning styles of his students—some of us, for example, learn by listening, while others of us learn by doing.

This was Peter's experience. In Matthew 15, Jesus is explaining what makes someone clean or unclean before God. "Listen and understand. What goes into someone's mouth does not defile them, but what comes out of their mouth, that is what defiles them" (Matthew 15:10-11). He is once again standing up against the Pharisees and the teachers of the Law who taught a system of dietary restrictions and ritualistic washings.

Take note as to who was listening to this explanation. In addition to the crowds, we are told that disciples were present and actively involved in the conversation, even asking questions (Matthew 15:12). That would include Peter. But apparently, as we'll see, Peter didn't understand the implications of what Jesus was teaching. Fast-forward many years, and we see that Jesus is still actively teaching Peter about cleanliness and uncleanliness before God (Acts 10).

> About noon the following day as they were on their journey and approaching the city, Peter went up on the roof to pray. He became hungry and wanted something to eat, and while the meal was being prepared, he fell into a trance. He saw heaven opened and something like a large sheet being let down to earth by its four corners. It contained all kinds of four-footed animals, as well as reptiles and birds. Then a voice told him, "Get up, Peter. Kill and eat."
>
> "Surely not, Lord!" Peter replied. "I have never eaten anything impure or unclean."
>
> The voice spoke to him a second time, "Do not call anything impure that God has made clean."
>
> This happened three times, and immediately the sheet was taken back to heaven.
>
> ACTS 10:9-16

Jesus wants Peter to go to a Gentile's house to explain the gospel, but Peter is still hung up on what is clean and unclean. So even years later, Jesus patiently works with his student until the lesson is learned. I love that Jesus doesn't say, "Don't you remember what I taught you? Why aren't you getting this?" Instead, Jesus patiently works with his student. Apparently, Peter needed to hear something at least three times before it clicked—remember how many times Jesus asked him, "Do you love me?" after his resurrection (John 21:15-19)? Here we are told that Jesus essentially put this video presentation on repeat: "This happened three times, and then it was all pulled up to heaven again" (Acts 11:10).

Peter was now ready to pass the test.

What if Jesus is also doing this in your life? Once Jesus is your rabbi, he is always your rabbi. He's patiently teaching you, taking into account your unique needs as a student. He's willing to repeat any lesson until you and I fully grasp it, enabling us to truly become who he has made us to be. Perhaps this is why you've read something in Scripture and then heard a song about the same thing on a later occasion. Or maybe you went to a movie with friends and were struck by how it corresponded with your pastor's sermon the week before. Jesus is doing the same thing with you that he did with Peter and the other original disciples.

So. What do you want to know? What do you want Jesus to teach you?

When the Student Is Ready

As Christians, we want to be like Jesus. We desire to think as Jesus would and react in a manner that resembles him. We want to speak words of life and to love selflessly. Christlikeness is important to us, but how do we increasingly become like Jesus?

One school of thought says that we become like Jesus by modeling our lives after him. Dallas Willard, in his book *The Spirit of the Disciplines: Understanding How God Changes Lives*, explains it this way: "We *can* become like Christ by doing one thing—by following him in the overall style of life he chose for himself."[3] The idea is that Jesus left us pathways to follow. When we do so, Willard says, "we can, through faith and grace, become like Christ by practicing the types of activities he engaged in, by arranging our whole lives around the activities he himself practiced in order to remain constantly at home in the fellowship of his Father."[4] Jesus fasted, so we fast. Jesus prayed, so we pray. We see a regular rhythm of solitude and silence in Jesus' life as he often withdrew from the crowds to spend time with his Father, and we should do the same.

There is great reward in modeling your life after Jesus. Following in the footsteps of Jesus brings us closer to him and his way of life. Paul calls us to "follow God's example, therefore, as dearly loved children" (Ephesians 5:1). This "imitation of Christ" approach has great value when it comes to training ourselves for godliness (1 Timothy 4:7). For example, when we fast during Lent, we vicariously enter into the temptations of Jesus when he was led by the Spirit to fast in the wilderness for forty days (Matthew 4:1-11; Luke 4:1-13). Such imitation establishes patterns of behavior—spiritual muscle memory, if you will—that we draw upon when needed.

Having said that, if we actually want to be like Jesus, we

can't stop here. This approach to Christlikeness still has us looking in the spiritual rearview mirror. It's still past tense in its perspective. Jesus, however, told us how to become like him in the present tense when he said, "The student is not above the teacher, but everyone who is fully trained will be like their teacher" (Luke 6:40).

We become like our teachers. Therefore, if Jesus is your teacher, then you will become like him. So the ultimate path to Christlikeness is to be discipled by Jesus himself.

Have you chosen Jesus as your teacher?

Have you ever wondered why the disciples had to ask Jesus to teach them to pray? Prayer is extremely important in our relationship with God. It's essential to a vibrant, meaningful relationship with him, but Jesus didn't take the initiative in teaching his disciples about this. Rather, they had to ask him for his teaching. In Luke 11 we are told that, "One day Jesus was praying in a certain place. When he finished, one of his disciples said to him, 'Lord, teach us to pray, just as John taught his disciples'" (Luke 11:1).

Jesus lived a prayer-dependent life. Luke remarks often about the prayer life of Jesus.

- "As he was praying, heaven was opened" (Luke 3:21).
- "At daybreak, Jesus went out to a solitary place" (Luke 4:42).
- "Jesus often withdrew to lonely places and prayed" (Luke 5:16).

- "One of those days Jesus went out to a mountainside to pray, and spent the night praying to God" (Luke 6:12).
- "He withdrew about a stone's throw beyond them, knelt down and prayed" (Luke 22:41).

Jesus prayed all of the time. Not only before big moments like his baptism, the feeding of the five thousand, or the choosing of his twelve disciples, but also as a normal part of life. Jesus was found praying late at night in the dark, early in the morning as the sun was rising, and in solitary, lonely places. Jesus was so passionate about prayer that he overturned the tables in the Temple and proclaimed, "My house will be a house of prayer" (Luke 19:46).

Yet, Jesus didn't teach his disciples how to pray. Other rabbis did. The disciples pointed out that even John had taught his disciples to pray. But it wasn't until they implored him, "Lord, teach us to pray" that Jesus delivered the perfect curriculum (complete with analogies, specific instructions, and the Lord's Prayer) for those who desire to talk to God (Luke 11:2-13). You don't get the sense that Jesus forgot to teach them these things. No, it seems like he was just waiting for them to ask.

This makes me wonder if Jesus is waiting for us to ask too. Not just about prayer but about everything. If we want to know something about life with God, Jesus is more than willing to answer our questions. What do you want to know about the spiritual life? Have you asked Jesus to teach you? Take your requests to Jesus:

Lord, teach us . . .

. . . to pray.

. . . to fight sin.

. . . to love our neighbors as ourselves.

. . . to bless those who curse us.

. . . to turn the other cheek.

. . . to forgive.

. . . to love unconditionally.

. . . to pick up our cross and follow you.

Lord, teach us.

What do you want him to teach you? Jesus is the greatest teacher, but he waits for us to walk into the classroom, take our seats, and raise our hands. Maybe the old adage is true: "When the student is ready, the teacher will appear."

Hopefully, by now you are seeing the incredible opportunity that is available to all of us. Jesus is ready, willing, and able to be your pastor and to teach you directly. You and I can be discipled by Jesus. But you're probably wondering how this all works. Practically, how can we be led, loved, and taught by Jesus even though he is not physically present with us? Let's now turn our attention to the role of the Holy Spirit in our experience of the risen Jesus today.

CHAPTER FIVE

LEARNING TO PRAY
in the Spirit

I deeply desire to see the body of Christ united across the divides of race, class, and culture. If you were to attend Colorado Community Church, where I pastor, you would see young and old, rich and poor, every race, and dozens of nations worshiping together. It's beautiful when God's people gather despite—perhaps even because of—their differences.

We're an *inter*-denominational church. That is, we love what happens when the various streams of Christianity—Baptist, Presbyterian, Catholic, Anglican, AME, Lutheran, and so on—flow toward each other so we can immerse ourselves in the vast richness of the body of Christ. We live and learn from one another. On any given weekend, you can experience vibrant R&B, gospel-infused music in our Worship Center, a singer/songwriter vibe in our "Upper Room," or a sacramental service where we worship Christ aided by ancient liturgies. And, of course, we sprinkle in a little jazz and hip-hop for fun.

Theologically, we follow the old adage: "In essentials unity, in nonessentials liberty, and in all things, love." This allows us to stand together on the crucial elements of our faith while not dividing over other important yet nonessential issues. Our desire for unity means that we recognize we are not competing with other churches in our city; this frees us to weave a fabric of friendship with them and to help grow fruit on others' trees. We truly believe that it takes the whole church to reach the whole city. No one church is enough. No one church can be all things to all people. We need one another.

Our focus on the larger body of Christ has led us to practice a unique way of giving. We call it 5 + 5. We ask our people to give at least 10 percent of their income to God—but not to give it all to our church. Instead, we ask that they give 5 percent to Colorado Community Church and the other 5 percent outside of our walls. I regularly say things like "Ask God where he wants the other half of your giving to go. Does he want you to give it to another church? Then give it there. What about supporting a missionary or adopting a struggling family in your neighborhood?" This makes the whole congregation the missions committee of the church! It's such a delight to watch our people—who have been discipled by Jesus—give money to the things that God has laid directly on their heart—teen mothers, the homeless, international missions, and orphan care, to name a few. Our congregation gives more to local, national, and international missions than we as church leadership ever would have budgeted. I believe this is why we have so many people serving in ministry.

According to Jesus, our hearts follow our money. Jesus said, "Where your treasure is, there your heart will be also" (Matthew 6:21). When people give to the church, their hearts are in the mission of the church, and when they personally give outside the walls, their hearts are there, also. We do this because we truly believe that we are not competing with other churches, that we are all part of the body of Christ. For us, it's a radical display of unity.

Meeting Pope Francis

A few years ago, Pope Francis—who deeply desires unity in the body of Christ—became aware of a remarkable movement toward unity among Protestants and Catholics in Phoenix, Arizona. They're known as the John 17 movement, based upon the prayer that Jesus prayed for us when he said,

> I pray also for those who will believe in me through
> their message, that all of them may be one, Father,
> just as you are in me and I am in you. . . . I in them
> and you in me—so that they may be brought to
> complete unity. Then the world will know that

you sent me and have loved them even as you have loved me.

JOHN 17:20-21, 23

After the pope's visit to the United States in 2015, representatives of the John 17 movement received a personal papal invitation to the Vatican for a conversation about unity and reconciliation. The goal was to start a healing dialogue between Catholics and Protestants. Given our hearts for unity in the body of Christ, my wife, Barbara, and I were ecstatic when the leadership of the John 17 movement asked us to join them in this meeting.

It wasn't until we arrived in Rome that we met our fellow travelers. In addition to those from Phoenix, there were a couple of dozen church leaders from California, Portland, Texas, and New York, as well as a handful of Pentecostal pastors from Italy. What we all had in common was a heart for unity among God's people.

We were given a day to get acclimated, and then we were treated to an amazing private tour of the Sistine Chapel and the Vatican. On the third day, we met with Pope Francis. Upon arriving at the Vatican, we were ushered past the Swiss guards, down long corridors, and into a cozy room. Our seats formed a horseshoe, all focused on a stately chair at the center of the opening. After a short wait, Pope Francis unassumingly walked into the room. He sat down and, like a gentle grandfather, began to make his remarks. "We are all concerned about the great scandal that Christians are not united."

Our meeting quickly turned into a worship service, as together we sang, "I Love You, Lord," prayed for each other, and enjoyed the dialogue. The formal meeting ended, and Pope Francis simply mingled, engaged in small talk, and posed for selfies. In all, we spent almost three hours together. It was an experience that Barbara and I will always cherish.

We stayed a few extra days in Rome in order to take in the beauty and history of the city. We found a favorite coffee shop and each morning sipped espresso at a bistro table on the sidewalk as we watched the hustle of morning commuters. At night, we strolled the ancient streets and held hands at Trevi Fountain. We stood awestruck outside the Pantheon—the site of what many say is the longest-active Christian congregation in the world. Soberly, we toured the Colosseum and considered the suffering that took place there.

We spent the longest amount of time at the Roman Forum across the street from the Colosseum, tucked in a valley at the foot of the Palatine Hill. In first-century Rome, this was Main Street. It was the business, governmental, and spiritual heart of the city. The ancient streets of the Forum are filled with the ruins of dozens of temples built for gods such as Venus, Saturn, and Caesar. It was here that a verse from 1 Corinthians came to mind, and I opened my small pocket Bible and read, "Do you not know that your bodies are temples of the Holy Spirit, who is in you, whom you have received from God?" (1 Corinthians 6:19).

Whether in Rome or Corinth, Christians daily walked by these massive temples dedicated to the gods . . . how that must have surprised those early Christians to learn that each of them was a temple of the Most High God. So, too, you and I are "temples of the Holy Spirit." This is an indispensable truth—the missing link—when it comes to experiencing the reality of being discipled by Jesus himself.

The Spirit Spotlights Jesus

After speaking at a retreat or to a congregation about being discipled by Jesus, I'm often asked about the role of the Holy Spirit. In these conversations, I've found that most people know that the Spirit is important to the Christian life but are confused about what he actually does in relation to their spiritual growth.

Many speak about the Holy Spirit as if he's the new sheriff in town, as if Jesus had his opportunity, and now it's the Spirit's turn. They don't actually say this, but their questions imply that Jesus now takes a back seat to the work of the Spirit. This couldn't be further from the truth.

As God's temples, we are "filled with the Spirit" (Ephesians 5:18). However, being full of the Spirit doesn't mean that we have less of Jesus. Quite the opposite, actually: To be full of the Spirit is to have more of Jesus than we ever thought was possible.

Jesus told us to "go and make disciples" (Matthew 28:19). As we'll see, this is not an invitation for us to collect disciples for ourselves but rather to enroll other people as his students so they can be discipled by Jesus himself. But notice that right after he told his disciples to "go," he instructed them to "wait."

Do not leave Jerusalem, but wait for the gift my
Father promised, which you have heard me speak
about. For John baptized with water, but in a few
days you will be baptized with the Holy Spirit.

ACTS 1:4-5

Before they were to go, Jesus told them to wait for the
gift. We are not to attempt to do Kingdom work without the
Spirit. To serve others in the way of God's Kingdom, we need
the Spirit. To grow spiritually ourselves, we need the Spirit.
Simply put, *the Holy Spirit is the gift our Father gives us so that
we might know his Son better and see him more clearly.*

As Christians, we believe in one God—"Hear, O Israel:
The LORD our God, the LORD is one" (Deuteronomy 6:4)—
who mysteriously and beyond our comprehension reveals
himself as a trinity: Father, Son, and Holy Spirit. When we
get to know God the Father, we discover that we can be
fathered by God. When we get to know God the Son and
grasp that he died on the cross for the redemption of all
creation, we discover that we can be discipled by Jesus. But
when we get to the Holy Spirit, there's much controversy and
misunderstanding.

The Holy Spirit is essential to our relationship with God,
for the Holy Spirit *is* God—fully God, coequal to the Father
and Son—and as such, the Trinity works together in our
discipleship. Jesus spent significant time teaching about who
the Spirit is and preparing us for the role he would play in
our lives. He referred to him as "the Advocate" (John 14:26).

That is, he's like our lawyer on permanent retainer. This would have meant a lot to Christians dealing with persecution. As they faced life-and-death trials and tribunals, they knew that they did not stand alone.

The Holy Spirit is with us. We, too, sense his empowering presence whenever you and I take the witness stand of life to give our testimony (Acts 1:8). Jesus promised us that the Spirit "will teach you all things and will remind you of everything I have said to you" (John 14:26). In these moments, our advocate brings comfort, encouragement, and guidance.

Jesus also said that the Holy Spirit is responsible for the conviction of sin (John 16:8). I'm so grateful for this. There have been many times in my life when I've sensed the Spirit grieving because of my choices (Ephesians 4:30). It's been the Spirit who brought about confession and repentance as he gently called me back to God's best for my life.

It can be tough watching our children spread their wings of freedom. We wonder if they will remember what we've taught them. We worry when we see them headed down the wrong path. Take heart, the Holy Spirit is on the job. We don't have to be the "Reminder in Chief" when it comes to right and wrong in our children's lives. The Holy Spirit is already doing that as he woos, convicts, and speaks directly to their souls, prodding our prodigals to come home.

In addition to all of this, the Spirit is intimately involved in our transformation as new creatures in Christ (2 Corinthians 5:17). As we let go of life in the flesh, it is the Spirit that brings about love, joy, peace, forbearance, kindness, goodness, faithfulness, gentleness, and self-control (Galatians 5:22-23). Paul also tells us that the Spirit assists us in our prayer life: He "intercedes for us through wordless groans" when "we do not know what we ought to pray for" (Romans 8:26).

Most Christians seem to be clear on these core truths. But we often fail to see the connection between the Holy Spirit and Jesus. It's true that the Spirit is continuing the mission of Jesus, but this doesn't mean that Jesus is stepping aside. Remember, *the Holy Spirit is the gift our Father gives us so that we might know his Son better and see him more clearly.*

This close connection between Jesus and the Spirit even caused Paul and Peter to combine them in title. In these passages, notice how the biblical writers refer to Jesus and the Spirit in tandem:

- "If anyone does not have the Spirit of Christ, they do not belong to Christ" (Romans 8:9).
- "Because you are his sons, God sent the Spirit of his Son into our hearts, the Spirit who calls out, '*Abba,* Father'" (Galatians 4:6).
- "Concerning this salvation, the prophets, who spoke of the grace that was to come to you, searched intently and with the greatest care, trying to find out the time and circumstances to which the Spirit of Christ in them was pointing when he predicted the sufferings of the Messiah and the glories that would follow" (1 Peter 1:10-11).

The Spirit and Jesus are distinct but intimately linked in the mission of God. In the same way Jesus revealed the Father to us—"If you really know me, you will know my Father as well. From now on, you do know him and have seen him" (John 14:7)—so the Spirit reveals Jesus to us.

Jesus made this clear when he said,

> [The Spirit] will not speak on his own; he will speak only what he hears, and he will tell you what is yet to come. He will glorify me because it is from me that he will receive what he will make known to you. . . . The Spirit will receive from me what he will make known to you.
>
> JOHN 16:13-15

Jesus said of the Holy Spirit, "He will glorify me." As the Father sent the Son and the Son brought glory to the Father, so the Son sends the Spirit and the Spirit brings glory to the Son. We need to wait for the Spirit because *the Holy Spirit glorifies the Son*.

The Spirit shines a massive spotlight on Jesus. He magnifies Christ in our lives. The Holy Spirit puts Jesus on display. Jesus is revealed to us by the Spirit. The Spirit delights in glorifying the Son, and this is how we are discipled by Jesus!

This work of illumination allows us to continue to see our risen rabbi as he works in our lives. The book of Revelation is a great place to observe the relationship between the Spirit and Jesus as it pertains to your discipleship. In the last book of the Bible, we see an explosion of Jesus' words fully aided by the Holy Spirit. Here the Spirit is operating in full force, and the result is that we see Jesus.

> I, John, your brother and companion in the suffering and kingdom and patient endurance that are ours in Jesus, was on the island of Patmos because of the word of God and the testimony of Jesus. On the Lord's Day I was in the Spirit, and I heard behind me a loud voice like a trumpet, which said: "Write on a scroll what you see and send it to the seven churches: to Ephesus, Smyrna, Pergamum, Thyatira, Sardis, Philadelphia and Laodicea."
>
> REVELATION 1:9-11

John is "in the Spirit" as he hears and sees Jesus. In Revelation, we see Jesus continuing the discipleship of his beloved friend and student.

It's real.

Experiential.

Up close.

Terrifying.

Breathtaking.

Because of the Holy Spirit, this, too, can be our experience of discipleship. Being discipled by Jesus is a Spirit-led and Spirit-empowered process for those who are filled with the Spirit. When we are "in the Spirit," we see Jesus.

Just Me and My Bible?

"What's your new book about?" the man asked.

"It's about how we all can be discipled by Jesus," I replied. He looked confused, so I continued, "What Jesus did for the twelve disciples, he can also do for you."

Looking like he had a light bulb moment, the man said, "Oh, you mean me and my Bible."

"No," I answered. "You and *Jesus!*"

Perhaps you're also wondering if that's what this is all about. Is this about spending more time reading your Bible? As important as the Bible is, being discipled by Jesus is so much more.

I love reading the Bible. It's essential to our walk with God, for in the Scriptures, we see Jesus revealed. On many occasions, Jesus indicated that all of the Bible is about him.

- "Do not think that I have come to abolish the Law or the Prophets; I have not come to abolish them but to fulfill them" (Matthew 5:17).
- "Beginning with Moses and all the Prophets, he explained to them what was said in all the Scriptures concerning himself" (Luke 24:27).
- "This is what I told you while I was still with you: Everything must be fulfilled that is written about me in the Law of Moses, the Prophets and the Psalms" (Luke 24:44).
- "You study the Scriptures diligently because you think that in them you have eternal life. These are the very Scriptures that testify about me" (John 5:39).

Reading the Bible is like a treasure hunt: We seek Jesus on every page. Because the Bible is so integral to our faith and understanding of Jesus, sometimes we think that discipleship is just sitting down and reading about Jesus. However, as important as God's Word is, being discipled by Jesus is more than a "me and my Bible" experience. The difference is this: In the Bible, we learn *about* Jesus. In discipleship, we learn *from* Jesus.

This is where the Holy Spirit comes in. When we return to Jesus and John in the book of Revelation, we see that the Holy Spirit was clearly at work. This is hinted at in the very title of the book. Revelation's name comes from its first verse, where we read these words: "The Revelation of Jesus Christ" (Revelation 1:1, NKJV). It's called "the Revelation" because something—some*one*—is being revealed, and that someone is Jesus. The resurrected Jesus was revealed to John in all of his glory.

> I turned around to see the voice that was speaking
> to me. And when I turned I saw seven golden
> lampstands, and among the lampstands was someone
> like a son of man, dressed in a robe reaching down
> to his feet and with a golden sash around his chest.
> The hair on his head was white like wool, as white
> as snow, and his eyes were like blazing fire. His feet
> were like bronze glowing in a furnace, and his voice
> was like the sound of rushing waters. In his right
> hand he held seven stars, and coming out of his

mouth was a sharp, double-edged sword. His face
was like the sun shining in all its brilliance.

REVELATION 1:12-16

Utterly astounding! It was such an overwhelming, other-
worldly experience that John collapsed to the ground. As he
did, Jesus drew even nearer:

When I saw him, I fell at his feet as though dead.
Then he placed his right hand on me and said: "Do
not be afraid. I am the First and the Last. I am the
Living One; I was dead, and now look, I am alive
for ever and ever!"

REVELATION 1:17-18

That's spiritual growth in light of the Resurrection! Jesus
up close, palpable, and personal.

In light of this, Peter's encounter with Jesus in Acts 10
no longer seems so exotic or farfetched. Peter tells us that it
happened when he "went up on the roof to pray" and "fell
into a trance" (Acts 10:9-10). Jesus then proceeded to teach
Peter directly. Peter seems to be describing the work of the
Spirit glorifying and revealing Jesus. The Holy Spirit helped
Peter to hear and understand what Jesus was teaching him.

Our souls are able to connect with Jesus aided by the
Spirit of Christ.

We see the same thing with the apostle Paul as Jesus actually stands next to him and speaks life-directing words and
gives him strength:

- "The following night the Lord stood near Paul and said, 'Take courage! As you have testified about me in Jerusalem, so you must also testify in Rome'" (Acts 23:11).
- "The Lord stood at my side and gave me strength, so that through me the message might be fully proclaimed and all the Gentiles might hear it" (2 Timothy 4:17).

These were mysterious and mystical encounters with Jesus. Paul said that he had "visions and revelations from the Lord," that he was "caught up to the third heaven . . . whether in the body or apart from the body I do not know, but God knows," and that he was "caught up to paradise and heard inexpressible things, things that no one is permitted to tell" (2 Corinthians 12:1-4). During one of these moments, Jesus famously said, "My grace is sufficient for you, for my power is made perfect in weakness" (2 Corinthians 12:9). Once more, I think Paul is recounting for us the revealing work of the Spirit as Jesus continues to disciple him directly.

Jesus is ready, willing, and able to engage you and me just like this. But how does this happen? How does the Holy Spirit help us see Jesus in this way? Revelation happens when we learn to pray the way John was praying.

Praying in the Spirit

How does the Holy Spirit facilitate a discipleship encounter with Jesus? John saw and heard Jesus directly, and Jesus' words flowed into his life. If we could understand how that happened with him, then maybe we could understand how this could happen with us.

John tells us exactly what he was doing when Jesus was revealed to him: "On the Lord's Day I was in the Spirit" (Revelation 1:10). That's how it happened. He was "in the Spirit," and that led to a face-to-face meeting with Jesus. If we could understand what "in the Spirit" means, then maybe we, too, could see and hear Jesus. For this is precisely the gift our Father gives us when we wait for the Spirit. Peter was praying, and he was discipled by Jesus himself. Stephen was a man "known to be full of the Spirit" (Acts 6:3), and he "saw the glory of God, and Jesus standing at the right hand of God" (Acts 7:55). When we are "in the Spirit," we see Jesus.

About a decade ago, I wanted to discover what this meant for myself. I hungered for a deeper knowledge and experience of Jesus and of the revealing work of the Holy Spirit. I knew about spiritual gifts (Romans 12:3-8; 1 Corinthians 12:1-11), and I'd learned the ways of the Spirit from my charismatic Pentecostal and Quaker brothers and sisters, but I was convinced that there was more. I wanted what could only be found in "the face of Christ" (2 Corinthians 4:6). I wanted to learn how to pray "in the Spirit."

I read A. W. Tozer, and he spurred me on when he wrote that Jesus "waits to be wanted. Too bad that with many of us He waits so long, so very long, in vain."[1]

My pursuit then led me to St. Ignatius, an early Christian who practiced a way of meeting Jesus in prayer through the power of the Spirit that resembles what we see with John in the Revelation.

And then I read a book called *Seeing Is Believing: Experience Jesus through Imaginative Prayer*, written by a pastor who draws heavily upon the Ignatian tradition. I knew he was onto something when I read,

> God didn't stop with sending his Son to dwell
> among us; he also sent his Spirit to reside within
> us. . . . The main work of the Holy Spirit, then, is
> not to supplement what the Son did but to *apply*
> what the Son did to the lives of God's people. He
> glorifies Christ by revealing him to his children. . . .
> He does not speak of himself . . . but rather causes
> people to behold the glory of the Lord in the face of
> Jesus Christ.[2]

Isn't that what we want? A Spirit-guided, face-to-face encounter with Jesus that resembles what we read about in Scripture? What I discovered was a well-worn path that Spirit-led people have walked for centuries. The promise at the end of this road is that others, aided by the Spirit, have found Jesus. That we can actually hear and perhaps even see Jesus.

If we desire to follow in these footsteps, here are three words, three signs that will mark the way: *rest, surrender, wait.*

Rest. Praying in the Spirit "requires discipline to carve out of our busy schedule a time to be alone with Christ. When we practice prayer or meditation only when we have 'spare time,' we end up praying and meditating very little. And even when we do, it is often not very focused and hence not very fruitful."[3] What's needed is a quiet place and a quiet hour. Pick a time. Pick a place.

John was on the island of Patmos. He was exiled there "because of the word of God and the testimony of Jesus" (Revelation 1:9). In his suffering, John was able to find silence and solitude. For me, I find my "soul rest" in the middle of the night. As the father of six children, it's not easy to find quiet space. Oftentimes, my house isn't restful until somewhere around midnight. So, late at night, when everyone is finally sleeping, I put my noise-canceling headphones over my ears and begin to worship through music. I praise and adore God and settle into my Father's love. Then I open God's Word and continue to find solace in the redemption story of Scripture.

Resting in God's presence takes practice but eventually your soul will find its quiet place. The goal is to be able to do as the psalmist described:

> I have calmed and quieted myself,
>> I am like a weaned child with its mother;
>> like a weaned child I am content.
>
> PSALM 131:2

Surrender. After rest comes surrender to the Spirit. Praying in the Spirit requires that we trust the Holy Spirit with our minds. At first, the idea of abdicating control of our minds sounds a bit scary, even if it's God that we're giving control to. But if you think about it, we give over control of our minds all the time to frivolous things. Remember that last time you binge-watched your favorite TV show to the point that it was all you could think about? Even these small, rather harmless activities impact the life of our minds greatly. Have you ever found yourself dreaming about the lives, relationships, and struggles of fictional characters? That's a kind of releasing control of your mind, and it's powerful. Sometimes we hand over control of our minds to images on our computer screens or fantasies in our heads that have no right to the amount of attention we afford them.

We know about surrendering control of our minds to lesser loves. Praying in the Spirit is about surrendering to a greater love—the Holy Spirit.

Our minds are powerful, especially when it comes to imagination. "Imagination is simply the mind's ability to evoke images of things that aren't physically present."[4] Right now think about a loved one who is not physically with you—imagine their eyes, laugh, voice—and represent them in your mind. "Notice the word 'represent'; it literally means 'to make present again.'"[5] When we use our minds to re-present someone, our emotions are evoked and our senses are awakened. In your mind, you can re-present your vacation to the beach and feel the water on your toes. Or you can call to mind the moment when you stood at the altar and said, "I do."

Imagination is powerful. When we imagine something, we feel. When we imagine something, we desire. When we imagine, we are inspired to action. Imagination is what allows us to experience that which is real even though it's not physically present.

So what if we surrendered control of this amazing ability to the Spirit of Christ? What if we used our imaginations in prayer? Praying "in the Spirit" takes place when we allow the Holy Spirit to re-present Jesus to us using our imaginations.

With my soul at rest, I then whisper a prayer to God, the Advocate, the Counselor, the Gift, the Spirit of Christ: "My mind is yours, all of my thoughts, all of the images, everything. Holy Spirit, I surrender to you. Sanctify my imagination. May the meditations of my heart be pleasing to you. Glorify Jesus now. Do what only you can do; show me the real Jesus. Reveal Jesus to me."

Then I sit still. "What happens after this is up to the Spirit."[6]

Sometimes Jesus arrives quickly. Other times, he's taken almost an hour. Most times, I don't see him, but I sense him.

It's here that the Spirit may employ some or all of your five senses. Once your soul is at rest and your mind is surrendered to the Spirit, *wait* for the Spirit to do what the Spirit does. Wait for him to reveal Jesus.

It helps to have an *inner sanctuary*.[7] Ask the Spirit to show you the place where Jesus wants to meet you. Remember, you can trust the Spirit of Christ. Cooperate with him. He might lead you to a place from your childhood where you felt especially safe or that special place in the woods that you visit often. It might be a place in Scripture; perhaps you sit among the crowds on the hillside as Jesus teaches or in a group as Jesus blesses a young boy's lunch and you begin to eat with the others. In your imagination, go there with him—let the Spirit of Christ lead you.

For me, the Spirit usually leads to me to get in the boat with Peter (John 21). I feel the waves swaying the boat. I watch as he throws the net overboard. There's a voice from the shore—we know it's Jesus. Peter splashes into the water; I'm close behind. I'm not a good swimmer in real life or in my imagination, but I arrive on the shore just in time to hear Jesus ask, "Do you love me?"

I smell the fish cooking. The fire warms me. I respond. "Yes, I love you."

I continue to wait. I'll admit, at times I wonder if it's him. But I trust the Spirit. I've asked him to sanctify my imagination and to re-present the real Jesus to me. And now he's here.

Most of the time, I sense his presence. Some of the time, I hear his voice. A few times, I've seen him. Through a glass darkly I've seen him, but I know it was him coming to me. He drew near in such a personal way. I know it was Jesus himself reaching, touching my soul, asking me if I want to be well. Yes, but well of what? Healed of what? He reaches down to that place in my heart where the memories hide from the light of day. All by the power of the Spirit.

Sometimes, he takes me back to painful places in my past to renew my mind (Romans 12:2). When this happens,

"Jesus does not literally change what happened in the past, of course. But he certainly changes its *message* to us in the present."[8]

Clouds and Rabbits

In these moments with Jesus at the campfire, Peter fades and it's just Jesus and me. Just the two of us. In the early days of meeting him this way, he spent significant time helping me with my childhood. There are things that I wished never happened to me, but I bear the scars proving that they did. Most of the time, the memories of these events reverberate like residual background noise, forgotten because of their familiarity. Sometimes, though, it feels like the volume is turned all the way up, and I can't ignore the facts. *Yes, I actually had to live through these things. They actually happened to me.*

One time when I was praying in the Spirit, Jesus came and sat with me. My heart was hurting from my past, and I was wondering how my life could have been different. Tears rolled down my cheek. He didn't say anything—rarely does.

But then suddenly, clouds rolled in and I was transported back to the moment where the grief started. I saw me, sitting in the living room when I was seven. Fear and shame flooded my heart, as if it were happening again.

Thankfully, Jesus was with me, then and now. It was as if time was suspended and the two moments were simultaneous. I don't know how to fully explain what happened. What I can tell you is that Jesus led *me* to *me*, and he gave me the opportunity to say anything I wanted to my seven-year-old self. I knelt down next to little Robbie, and after looking into his eyes, knowing all that was to come for him, I said, "Never forget that God is your daddy and that Jesus is with you."

The clouds lifted. I sat alone, headphones on my head. Discipled by Jesus himself.

Another time, I was at Glen Eyrie, a breathtaking conference center on the outskirts of Colorado Springs. Owned by The Navigators, it's known for its majestic mountains, bighorn sheep, wild turkeys, and a magnificent Tudor-style castle that sits in the midst of this eight-hundred-acre haven of rest.[9] It's one of my favorite places to go for a personal retreat. That afternoon, I checked in at the front desk and headed to my room. When I opened the door, I sensed a familiar presence. It was as if Jesus was already there. So I set my bags on the bed, dropped to my knees . . .

Resting.

Surrendering.

Waiting.

Praying in the Spirit.

He drew near. I had gone on this retreat with hopes that God would bring further healing in my life. I never knew my father, and in my early twenties, my persistent dream of finding him—for reasons I can't share—died. As I described earlier, God became my daddy, and I'm forever grateful. However, there were times during the following years when the pain returned. On this trip, I was hoping for some relief from the ache in my heart, and that's why I thought Jesus was there. But he had other plans.

We sat together for a while when I felt the urge to sing the old spiritual "Sometimes I Feel Like a Motherless Child." As I sang, my heart ruptured at an unfathomable depth. I curled up and sobbed on the floor. Why was this happening? I love my mom. We have a great relationship.

I then heard Jesus say, "We can be your mother, too."

Not understanding, I asked, "What does that mean?"

He gently reminded me of a truth that I had ignored all of my life. It's amazing how we can know facts but not face them, not really know their meaning. I love my mom, and today we are close. But Jesus wanted me to deal with a fundamental question of my early life: Why did my grandmother raise me? Where was my mom? She disappeared from life when I was two years old for understandable reasons that don't need to be rehearsed here; she didn't return until I was twelve. For a chunk of my childhood, I was motherless.

"We can be your mother, too."

Why not? If God can be my father and make up for what I missed out on not having a daddy, then surely he could fill the void left by those years when my mom was absent. God tells us that "as a mother comforts her child, so will I comfort you" (Isaiah 66:13). That night, the Holy Spirit re-presented Jesus to me so that Jesus could do for me what he did for countless unnamed people years ago when he walked the earth. It was real, and it was him.

I then remembered that I once heard someone say they asked God for something special, a moment just between the two of them. Something that whenever that person saw it would serve as a reminder of their relationship with God. Kind of like Stargazer lilies. That was the first flower I gave Barbara when we were dating, so whenever we see them, they are a reminder of that season of our relationship. I decided to give it a shot, and I asked Jesus for something special to remind me of the moments we had shared and the healing he had brought about in my life.

His answer made me laugh out loud. "Rabbits." My mom has a small tattoo of a rabbit just above her knee. It was now dark outside. Exhausted but fulfilled, I crawled into bed and went to sleep.

I woke early the next morning and decided to go on a hike. As I headed down one of the many trails, I looked up, and there was a rabbit sitting on the path a few yards in front of me. It thumped the ground and ran away. I continued, and as I turned the next corner, the rabbit was there, staring back at me. Again, it thumped and ran. This "game" continued for a few more minutes. It was a blast. I couldn't stop smiling. I no longer felt like a motherless child!

Praying in the Spirit is not a formula. Your experiences will be as unique to you as mine are to me. We can't replicate someone else's encounter with Christ any more than we could see the same vision that John saw of Jesus. Surrender to the Spirit's leading. Let him re-present Jesus to you as he sees fit. Trust the Spirit of Christ to reveal Jesus to you.

CHAPTER SIX

JOINING

the Great Co-Mission

In 1899, magazine editor Louis Klopsch read these words from the Gospel of Luke: "This cup is the new covenant in my blood, which is poured out for you" (Luke 22:20). He was struck by the potential symbolism of the blood of Christ and asked his mentor if he thought that a Bible with the words of Jesus in red might be a good idea. His friend replied, "It could do no harm and it most certainly could do much good." Thus, the Red Letter edition of the Bible was born.[1]

While all of the Scriptures are God's Word, the red letters highlight the words of Jesus in a unique way. The majority of red letters are concentrated in the four Gospels, which contain the accounts of Christ's teaching and interactions with people. This is to be expected. But crack open a Red Letter edition Bible to Acts 9, and you'll see something remarkable—the red letters continue!

> Saul was still breathing out murderous threats against the Lord's disciples. He went to the high priest and asked him for letters to the synagogues in Damascus, so that if he found any there who belonged to the Way [that is, followers of Christ], whether men or women, he might take them as prisoners to Jerusalem. As he neared Damascus on his journey, suddenly a light from heaven flashed around him. He fell to the ground and heard a voice say to him, "Saul, Saul, why do you persecute me?"
>
> "Who are you, Lord?" Saul asked.
>
> "I am Jesus, whom you are persecuting," he replied. "Now get up and go into the city, and you will be told what you must do."
>
> ACTS 9:1-6

It's not a surprise to see red letters in the Gospels because those books record the earthly ministry of Jesus. But what is astonishing is that after Jesus rose from the dead and ascended into heaven, the red letters didn't come to an end. Why? Because Jesus continued to disciple people himself! Which means the red letters can also show up on the pages of your life.

In Acts 9, we see Jesus clearly in charge of the soon-to-be

apostle Paul's conversion as he blinds him with a bright light, knocks him to the ground, and inquires why he's hell-bent on persecution. Jesus then instructs Saul to "get up and go into the city, and you will be told what you must do." Not only was Jesus present and fully engaged in Saul's conversion but later in the chapter, we see that Jesus also wants to disciple Saul: "I will show him how much he must suffer for my name" (Acts 9:16).

A brief study of Paul's life reveals that Jesus was indeed his rabbi. Jesus directly led him through a one-on-one discipleship process as he frequently revealed spiritual truths that specifically related to Paul's Kingdom calling.[2] Jesus even wanted to be the one to tell Paul about the suffering he was going to face, for the cross is essential to being a disciple of Jesus. Paul's life after his conversion was a vibrant, present-tense, interactive relationship with Jesus.

Don't get caught up in thinking that this kind of relationship was reserved only for Paul. We need to avoid the temptation of thinking that Paul was a super apostle and the rest of us need not get our hopes up when it comes to having the kind of relationship that he had with Jesus. Paul was special, but his experience of Jesus was not.

The red letters indicate that Jesus continues to be intimately involved not only in our conversion but also in our spiritual growth. As I stated earlier, any definition of discipleship that does not recognize this misses the point. *Discipleship is a direct, one-on-one relationship in which we are called by, led by, filled by, and taught by Jesus himself.* This kind of relationship with Jesus wasn't just for the twelve apostles. We see this here with Paul and many others; Jesus discipled people who were not part of the original group. Even after he had ascended into heaven, red letters continued to flow into people's lives because Jesus was—no, Jesus IS—the master disciple maker!

Notice how possessive Jesus was of Saul: "This man is my chosen instrument to proclaim my name" (Acts 9:15). Jesus says, "He's mine. I claim him. I have designs and plans for his life." For good reasons, most people wanted to keep Paul at a safe distance, but Jesus engaged and drew near so he could love, lead, and teach Paul directly. Jesus envisions the same kind of intimate—proprietary—relationship with you.

God has placed many people in your life to assist you in your walk with him. But you must not settle for anyone less than Jesus to be in charge of your discipleship. Only Jesus is qualified to give the Kingdom reasons for our birth, life, joys, and pains. When it comes to discipleship, this is the better way, the one that Mary chose and Jesus commended (Luke 10:42).

There are many factors that keep us from this better way of being discipled. Sometimes it's our questions driven by doubts and fears of unworthiness. Or perhaps it's an anti-supernatural bias that clouds our expectation of what is possible for us to experience. If you live only by what you can see, taste, and touch, then the idea of being discipled by Jesus may sound too mystical.

For some of us, it's not our divorce, addiction, or inability to embrace the mysterious that keeps us from the better way but our past spiritual achievements. If you've completed a rigorous program of Bible reading, memorization, and workbooks, then you might feel like you can check the "I have been discipled" box off the list of things you need to do in your Christian walk.

Perhaps the biggest barrier to this better way is a misunderstanding of the great commission.

Lost in Translation: It's a Verb

What did Jesus actually mean when he told us to "go and make disciples" (Matthew 28:19)? At first glance, Jesus' words seem absolutely clear, but sometimes the "obvious" is not so obvious. Sometimes things get lost in translation.

At first glance, it appears that Jesus is telling you and me that we—ourselves—are to "make disciples." However, two important nuances become evident when we consider these words in the original language.

First, in Greek, "make disciples" is only one word— *matheteuo*. It literally means "student." Second, this one word is a verb. There are other verbs in the great commission—*go*, *baptize*, and *teach*—that translate easily into English, but *matheteuo* is a bit more difficult and this is where we get off track.

After two millennia, we have allowed this verb to morph into an invented noun—*discipleship*. As I pointed out previously, *discipleship* is a word we Christians use all the time, but our definition of the word is actually not included in the dictionary. It's a word we've coined to describe the things we think Jesus is asking us to do in the great commission. If we are going to truly embrace what Jesus was actually saying, we first need to unlearn what we think he meant regarding this thing we call discipleship.

While it's extremely important that we teach people the story of the Bible and the essentials of the faith, we need to be careful not to confuse those activities with what Jesus meant when he said "make disciples." As we'll see with the rest of the great commission, knowing Scripture, giving our money, and attending church are vitally important to our Christian walk. But equating these activities with *discipleship* may actually keep us from Jesus' original intent. As important as these skills and competencies are, we must ask, "Are they what Jesus was asking us to do when he said 'make disciples'?"

Let's back up a little. *Matheteuo* is the word "student" in verb form. Jesus was literally telling us to "go into all the world and student the nations." That sounds a little clunky, so it makes sense why translators have tried to smooth it out by rendering it "make disciples." However, I believe that we have a better option when it comes to word choice. There is another a word that fits the context perfectly—*enroll*.[3]

Jesus is saying, "Here's what I want you to do. Go enroll people in school with me as their rabbi. I will be their teacher." We make disciples when we make students of Jesus. It's not about recruiting more people into our programs and classrooms but using all that's at our disposal to convince people to enroll with Jesus so they can be directly discipled by the master.

The difference is subtle, but extremely significant. Think about it this way. How would you make a disciple of a rabbi in the first century? The answer to that question would have depended on one key factor: Is your rabbi dead or alive? If your rabbi told you to go enroll people—that is, make disciples—how you responded depended upon whether your rabbi was currently available to potential students. If he was dead, then everything was on your shoulders. You were responsible for remembering and conveying his teachings to new students. However, if your rabbi was alive, then it was your job to recruit, prepare, and bring potential students to your rabbi.

Here's why all of this is so important: Jesus, our rabbi, is alive. He is risen; he has risen indeed! Therefore, he is not asking us to take on the primary role in someone's spiritual development. No, Jesus has asked us to enroll people in school with him. In the great commission, Jesus is essentially employing us as his admissions office. Our primary task is that of *preparing* people to be taught, led, and loved directly by Jesus.

As the church, we are to see ourselves as the ones who recruit and ready people to meet personally with their rabbi. We have dual roles as students of Jesus who also serve as his recruitment team. When we view ourselves this way, it radically alters the role we seek to have in someone's life. It never crosses the minds of those who work in a college admissions office that they are actually the professor! Church is to be the place and the people who prepare you to be discipled by Jesus himself.

Let's return to Jesus and Saul in Acts 9. Here we have Jesus initiating the spiritual birth *and* discipleship of Saul. On the road to Damascus, Jesus shined his light into Saul's life, knocked him to his knees, and asked, "Saul, Saul, why do you persecute me?" Saul was blinded, and as his world turned dark, he was faced with the reality that everything in his life must change, so he began to fast (Acts 9:1-9).

Concurrently, Jesus appeared in a vision to a man by the name of Ananias. He said, essentially, "Ananias, I want to invite you into something very special. I want you to join me in what I'm doing in Saul's life. Ananias, I need you to be present as Saul moves from darkness to light; it's a holy and sacred moment. Be present with us."

For good reason, Ananias was apprehensive. Saul was responsible for the killing of Stephen and was in pursuit of all Christians. Ananias feared prison, bodily harm, and even death. "But the Lord said to Ananias, 'Go! This man is my chosen instrument to proclaim my name to the Gentiles and their kings and to the people of Israel. I will show him how much he must suffer for my name'" (Acts 9:15-16).

Did you catch it? Jesus said, "Go." This is actually the second time "go" appears in this brief vision. In verse 11, Jesus said, "Go to the house of Judas on Straight Street." He repeated it here in verse 15. We last heard Jesus say "go" in the great commission. What we have here, then, is a case study demonstrating what Jesus meant when he said "Go . . . make disciples." Go . . . *enroll* people.

By the way, the church went for 1,600 years without

having a title for this passage in Matthew 28. Then, apparently, there was a German follower of Christ who, recognizing the magnitude of these words of Jesus, called it "the great commission." This name didn't catch on until Hudson Taylor popularized the term two hundred years later. Today, it's the assumed title for these essential words of Jesus. It's a good moniker, though it does come with an unintended image.[4]

How do you envision the great commission? Often, we imagine it as a relay race. As if Jesus ran his leg and has handed the baton to us. When that's our view, then we think it's our job to receive the baton, hold on tight, and run our leg as hard as we can.

Is that a correct way of thinking? Is the great commission a relay race? If it is, then Jesus is now simply on the infield of the track, cheering us on. However, what we have already seen is that quite the opposite is true, for he said, "I am with you always, to the very end of the age" (Matthew 28:20). Jesus is still running hard. Fully engaged. With us.

The great commission is actually a great "co-mission."

Jesus hasn't handed the baton to us and become a spectator. Rather, he's inviting us to join him. He's not watching us run away alone without him as he heads to the infield or waits for us at the finish line as we run our leg of the race. No, he's right beside us the whole way. We need a different metaphor for this co-mission that Jesus has invited us into.

Rather than a relay race, it's more like a three-legged race. Remember field day back in elementary school? You and your best friend would tie together the ankles and thighs of your inside legs and you were ready to run the race—together. Running a three-legged race isn't easy, is it? Success depends upon pre-race strategizing, coordination, and communication. The contestants need to agree on which leg they'll start with and the pace at which they'll proceed. They might even practice moving in sync with each other—"inside legs . . . outside legs . . . inside . . . outside"—so that when the race starts, they don't fall flat on their faces.

The same is true in our partnership with Jesus. If the great commission is actually a great co-mission, then when Jesus says, "go and make disciples," he is actually saying, "Let *us* go and make disciples. We're doing this together. You are not on your own."

If that's the case, then just like a three-legged race, the great commission requires much communication and coordination with our partner. He's not handing the baton off; therefore, we must coordinate, practice, and communicate so that we can move forward in harmony. When it comes to this co-mission, we need to be in sync with Jesus. Participating in the spiritual growth of people requires clarity in our coordination. *What are the things Jesus is asking us to do? What does Jesus want to do himself?*

What's So Amazing about Ananias

In Acts 9, we see Jesus fully engaged in Saul's conversion and discipleship. Even so, he invited a reluctant Ananias to join him in the process.

In Damascus there was a disciple named Ananias. The Lord called to him in a vision, "Ananias!"

"Yes, Lord," he answered.

The Lord told him, "Go to the house of Judas on Straight Street and ask for a man from Tarsus named Saul, for he is praying. In a vision he has seen a man named Ananias come and place his hands on him to restore his sight."

"Lord," Ananias answered, "I have heard many reports about this man and all the harm he has done to your holy people in Jerusalem. And he has come here with authority from the chief priests to arrest all who call on your name."

But the Lord said to Ananias, "Go!"

ACTS 9:10-15

Ananias was terrified and must have wondered, *Why me?* It is curious. What did Jesus see in him? Of all the people Jesus could have asked to participate in Saul's discipleship, why this man?

I like to think that the reason has to do with the phenomenon known as imprinting—the process that some animals use to immediately identify their parents at birth. For example, upon hatching from their eggs, many species of birds immediately latch on to the first moving object they see. That latching is imprinting, and it bonds those newly hatched birds to their actual mother and father or, at times, the family dog or whatever human happens to be present at the moment when they emerge from their eggs (which is why you occasionally see online videos of little ducklings following Labrador retrievers everywhere they go).

Illumination in the Flatwoods is the fascinating story of a man who decided to become a member of a gang of turkeys through imprinting. Joe Hutto, a wildlife artist, was interested in discovering more about the secret lives of elusive wild turkeys. To accomplish this, Hutto incubated two dozen eggs, keeping them warm and speaking to them through their shell. Hutto writes of the crucial moment when one hatchling emerged:

> For a moment the little wild turkey lies motionless and helpless, striving to catch his breath. I remember to make a sound. Speaking softly, just above a whisper, I make a feeble attempt to console him in what seems to be a desperate and confusing moment. Instantly, he raises his shaking wet head and looks me square in the eyes. In that brief moment I see a sudden and unmistakable flash of recognition in the little bird. Something completely unambiguous transpires in our gaze, and I am certain that the young turkey absolutely knows who I am.[5]

Such an amazing moment. As each wild turkey hatched, Hutto was present, and with the imprinting complete he was able to spend virtually every waking moment with the four males and ten females that survived to adulthood. They allowed him to be a part of their daily routine as they shared meals, napped, and went on walks together. He was accepted as one of them; man and wild turkeys became family.

Hutto's experiment wasn't without confusion or controversy. For starters, when the young male turkeys grew up, they saw him as competition during mating season. There were a few scuffles as the males attacked him in an attempt to secure the hens for themselves! Also, some naturalists criticized his tinkering with the imprinting process by unnaturally introducing a human element. For example, in situations such as the California Condor Project, humans put a condor puppet on their hand when interacting with young hatchlings so the young birds don't become confused about their own species.

Without pushing this analogy too far, I would like to suggest that there are some lessons we can learn from the imprinting process. You and I are the *body of Christ* (1 Corinthians 12:12-31), and when people "hatch" spiritually, we get to be present at those sacred moments. When we clothe ourselves in Christ (Romans 13:14), they see Jesus in us.

I love how Eugene Peterson calls us to embrace *The Jesus Way*.[6] In all of our activities, we imperfectly seek to resemble Jesus. Just as newborns are highly impressionable and will often begin to emulate and even imitate their closest early connections, people who are new to the faith are susceptible to the character we present to them. It's our task, as far as possible, to reflect Jesus and steer people toward Jesus, so they imprint on Jesus and not us. We embody Jesus as we raise our children, conduct business, and chat with our neighbors so others see a reflection of the characteristics and ways of Jesus. As the body of Christ, we intentionally take on Jesus' way of sharing the gospel, teaching the Scriptures, and loving the least of these so as to resemble our rabbi.

In Acts, we read that those opposing the early church noticed something about the first disciples of Jesus: "When they saw the courage of Peter and John and realized that they were unschooled, ordinary men, they were astonished and they took note that these men had been with Jesus" (Acts 4:13).

Certain characteristics that the disciples had in common with Jesus caused even their enemies to take note that they "had been with Jesus." Wanting to discover what these note-worthy characteristics might be, I read through the New Testament and wrote down as many adjectives as I could to describe Jesus. I then did the same for disciples in the early church. With pages of notes, I compiled and compared the two lists. There were obvious descriptors that were only true of Jesus. For example, Jesus was divine and the disciples were not. The disciples were sinful but Jesus was sinless. After eliminating these, I began to look for the overlap. Over time, I refined and word-smithed these into five phrases that have inspired me for years.

- Worship-Driven
- Spirit-Led
- Prayer-Dependent
- Grace-Centered
- Kingdom-Obsessed

These phrases capture for me what was true of Jesus *and* the early church. These traits have become the "Imprint Statement" of the church where I serve. They are as important to us as our Mission Statement and Statement of Faith. Our desire is for these to be the ethos of all we do, so when people experience spiritual birth in our presence, they experience Christ embodied in us and through us. The more time we spend with Jesus, the more we hope to exhibit this kind of life.

There are a variety of reasons why Jesus will call on you. Nothing in your life is coincidental. Pay attention to why you cry during certain movies and the specific people groups you are drawn to. There may even be small, seemingly unimportant things in your life that you've taken for granted, yet they may be the very reason why Jesus chooses you to join him in what he's doing in someone's life.

Let's bring this back to Ananias. For Ananias, it was his name.

Paul is sitting in blind darkness. Like Ananias, he, too, is afraid, his future uncertain. He's coming to terms with the reality that he has, in fact, been persecuting Jesus (Acts 9:4). In later years, he will call himself the "worst" of all sinners (1 Timothy 1:15). As he considers his self-righteous past, guilt and shame flood his soul. What he needs most is a tangible expression of the grace of God. He needs to know God loves him, and that there's nothing he can do about it!

I think this is the reason why Jesus chose Ananias. For "Ananias" literally means "The Lord shows grace"!

Imagine how this encounter might have occurred. Saul sits praying, grieving his sin.

Knock. Knock.

"Who is it?" Paul asks.

The voice on the other side of the door replies back, "It's Ananias"—The Lord Shows Grace.

Amazing! God's grace knocked on Paul's door!

When Saul opened the door to Ananias, he opened the door to the grace of God. With Ananias, the grace of God walked into the room. Days before, Saul would have sought to arrest this man, but now, this man says,

> "Brother Saul, the Lord—Jesus, who appeared to
> you on the road as you were coming here—has sent
> me so that you may see again and be filled with the
> Holy Spirit."
>
> Immediately, something like scales fell from Saul's
> eyes, and he could see again.
>
> ACTS 9:17-18

The first thing that Saul saw as a new creature in Christ—a spiritual hatchling—was Ananias: The Lord Shows Grace. Imprinted.

This imprint had a profound effect on the apostle Paul. He would go on to become a herald for the grace of God. Philip Yancey points out in his book *What's So Amazing about Grace?* that Paul "never recovered from the impact of grace:

the word appears no later than the second sentence in every one of his letters."[7]

Ananias was not a haphazard inclusion, and neither are you.

If you and I don't distinguish our role from Jesus', then we are not going to be effective in that moment when Jesus invites us, like Ananias, into the room. Thankfully, Jesus is clear as to what he wants us to do. As we go with him, he wants us to "baptize" and "teach" as we enroll people in school with Jesus as their rabbi. These are the prerequisites to being discipled by Jesus, so let's turn our attention to the significance of baptism and why Jesus asks us to focus our teaching on his commands. What it comes down to is this: Jesus is asking us to prepare potential disciples for the reality of the cross and to show them what it truly means to love God.

CHAPTER SEVEN

PREPARING PEOPLE
to Be Discipled by Jesus

As much as I'd like for us to turn our attention to other verbs in the great commission—*baptize* and *teach*—we can't quite yet. I'll unpack the beauty of those commands in a moment, for they are essential to our mission as God's people. But first, there is a huge, complicating factor that we must recognize.

The hard truth is this: The vast majority of Christians aren't ready to be discipled by Jesus.

Think for a moment about what was true of the original twelve disciples before they were discipled by Jesus. What was their pre-discipleship reality? Before the Twelve met Jesus, they already knew the Scriptures, had a God-centered world-view, attended worship services on a weekly basis, and, on average, were giving 23 percent of their income to the work of God.[1] When Jesus called them to be his disciples, he didn't have to get them up to speed. There was a preestablished foundation that Jesus was building upon.

The Twelve were raised as Jews, and this meant they were taught to read and write using the Torah at the age of five. They were steeped in a culture that assumed certain truths about God. Jesus didn't have to teach them remedial basics because they already had a working knowledge of Scripture and the ways of God. Thus, when Jesus called them to follow and they did so "at once" and "without delay" (Mark 1:18, 20), it wasn't because they were irresponsible or because business was bad or a midlife crisis was fueling their need for adventure. *They were ready* to be discipled by Jesus.

It's important for me to take a moment and point out what I'm not saying. I'm not saying that there are prerequisites that we have to meet in order to be saved. Salvation is the work of Christ alone on our behalf. "For it is by grace you have been saved, through faith—and this is not from yourselves, it is the gift of God" (Ephesians 2:8). I'm not talking about salvation—how we come to Jesus to be saved—but rather, how we come to Jesus after we are saved. I'm also not saying that there are a bunch of hoops we have to jump through before we can start meeting with Jesus. No, Jesus is available to all, regardless of how we come to him. That being said, it is important to note that the original disciples, by virtue of their upbringing and culture, were at a different starting point than we are.

Their pre-laid foundation wasn't perfect. Jesus had to help them unlearn preconceived notions about God and deprogram them of wrong assumptions about righteousness and Scripture. That being said, my point is that Jesus didn't have to start from scratch. Jesus built upon their baseline of preparation to disciple them for his coming Kingdom.

This baseline of readiness disappeared when the gospel started to reach people without an understanding of the basics. You can sense Paul's frustration when he writes to the Corinthian Christians:

> Brothers and sisters, I could not address you as people who live by the Spirit but as people who are still worldly—mere infants in Christ. I gave you milk, not solid food, for you were not yet ready for it. Indeed, you are still not ready.
>
> 1 CORINTHIANS 3:1-2

The preponderance of Christians do not have a working knowledge of the Bible, a commitment to the mission of the church, or a wallet that already demonstrates Kingdom generosity. Therefore, it is essential that churches spend a great deal of their resources to get their people up to speed on the basic discipleship prerequisites. It is a necessity that we coach people in the basic essentials of the faith and mentor them toward a discipleship relationship with Jesus.

The early church would require new converts to go through instruction designed to get them up to speed. At times, this happened for a season prior to their baptism, in which they mastered the basics and learned essential creeds of our faith.

Bridging this readiness gap is time consuming and, at times, unfruitful and disheartening. Because of this, it's just easier to call all of our readiness programming "discipleship," even though we know in our hearts that the ultimate goal is for people to have a genuine one-on-one interactive relationship with Jesus himself. This is how we got off course and ended up in the discipleship driver's seat. But it can change with us.

What if each of us took personal responsibility for our own readiness? What if we started asking ourselves questions like "Can Jesus assume the same baseline of preparation in my life as he did with the original Twelve?" and "Have I prepared myself to be discipled by Jesus?" These kinds of questions would have a drastic impact.

In my book *Finding the Groove*, I sought to make the case for seeing ourselves as "practicing Christians."[2] In a jazz ensemble, baseline knowledge and skill is assumed. It is assumed that you know your instrument, have memorized the basic songs, and have practiced. As a result, ensembles are ready to perform, ready to put that baseline knowledge and skill into action. Can you imagine how similar assumptions could change what you expected of others and what was expected of you at church? Imagine how conversations about discipleship would go if everyone involved were proficient and experienced in the essentials of the faith? I don't mean that we should necessarily expect mastery. Nor is expecting flawlessness reasonable. *But* a basic understanding of the essential grooves and riffs of the faith is powerful.

Ask any accomplished musician how they became proficient, and they will point to long, lonely hours of repetition—time spent playing scales, learning chords, and training fingers to move from one progression to another. Any skill requires that we spend the necessary time working on the fundamentals. Jazz musicians call it "time in the woodshed."

The woodshed can't be forced on someone; it has to be desired. If the average Christian would choose the woodshed and begin to practice the faith, everything would change. The things we've been calling discipleship are, from a first-century perspective, *pre*-discipleship. That is, this knowledge and skill is mere preparation for actually being discipled by Jesus.

Intentionally calling ourselves practicing Christians inspires us to approach commitment to Christ with passion and intentionality. This frees up the church to focus on what Jesus actually asked us to do: baptize and teach.

Baptize: Prepared for the Cross

Hearing that Jesus invites you to be present as he transforms someone's life might have you asking, "Why me?" Ananias likely wondered the same thing, and let me assure you that Jesus picked him (and has chosen you) for a reason. As we saw,

God is not random in these defining moments. Let's continue with our living case study of the great co-mission by noticing that upon arriving at the house where Saul was staying, one of the first things Ananias did was to baptize him: "Immediately, something like scales fell from Saul's eyes, and he could see again. He got up and was baptized" (Acts 9:18).

Baptism directly links discipleship to the Cross, and the Cross, I believe, is why many new believers become disillusioned with the Christian life. Oftentimes, when we invite people to become Christians, we don't give them a full picture of what's in store for them. We focus on all the benefits of asking Jesus into their hearts as we help them understand that their sins are forgiven and eternal life is theirs. In the process, we leave people ill-prepared for when they actually meet Jesus and when he hands them their own cross.

- He called the crowd to him along with his disciples and said: "Whoever wants to be my disciple must deny themselves and take up their cross and follow me" (Mark 8:34).
- "Whoever does not carry their cross and follow me cannot be my disciple" (Luke 14:27).

Baptism is a powerful symbol given to us by Jesus. It reminds us that in Christ, we can start over, that we have been cleansed from our sins. Even more, it prepares new believers for the reality of bearing a cross. Its importance lies in the tangible, unambiguous way that it immerses people in the life of the Cross. If you've been baptized, then you know this to be true. It's a visceral, experiential symbol of what we are saying yes to with our will and our lives.

Maybe you weren't told this when you were baptized or perhaps you just didn't hear the connection, but it's essential that we connect the dots between baptism and the cross. In baptism, we become a sermon to those who are present as we are submerged in the water. In that moment, we aren't just saying we believe that Jesus died and rose. We're saying that, *and* we are also communicating to all watching that *we too* are choosing to die—literally and figuratively—with the hope of new life. Therefore, Jesus is asking us to take the lead in preparing people for this actuality. When we baptize someone, we are preparing them for and—in a sense—warning them about the cross. To be baptized is to recognize that the cross is the crux of a discipleship relationship with Jesus. This is what Dietrich Bonhoeffer called the cost of discipleship.

> Just as Christ is Christ only in virtue of his suffering and rejection, so the disciple is a disciple only in so far as he shares his Lord's suffering and rejection and crucifixion. Discipleship means adherence to the person of Jesus, and therefore submission to the law of Christ which is the law of the cross.[3]

In addition to recognizing that the cross is essential to a discipleship relationship with Jesus, Bonhoeffer also pointed out that baptism is the seminal practice in our preparation.

The call of Christ, his baptism, sets the Christian
in the middle of the daily arena against sin and the
devil. Every day he encounters new temptations,
and every day he must suffer anew for Jesus Christ's
sake. The wounds and scars he receives in the fray
are living tokens of this participation in the cross of
his Lord.[4]

Bonhoeffer's understanding of the call of the cross could
explain why he saw the need to stand against Hitler when
many Christians failed to do so. How is it that so many
Christians living in Nazi Germany didn't see that following
Jesus meant opposing the extermination of Jewish people
while young Bonhoeffer not only stood against but ended
up giving his life for his resistance?

Dr. Reggie Williams says that Bonhoeffer was able to
make the connection between standing with Christ and
against Hitler in large part due to the time he spent in
Harlem, where he saw the cross as a lived reality among dis-
enfranchised people and not just an intellectual concept.
Williams describes this crossroads in Bonhoeffer's life:

After his pastorate in Barcelona, Bonhoeffer
spent a year writing his second dissertation. With
it completed, he sensed that he had problems
within his theology. Prior to his trip to New York,
Bonhoeffer confessed his growing uneasiness with
academic theology: "I feel in general that academic

work will not hold me for long." Bonhoeffer
later recalled his pre-New York career and wrote,
"I had not yet become a Christian but, wildly and
undisciplined, [I] was my own master."[5]

Arriving in the United States, Bonhoeffer initially didn't
find the authentic expression of Christianity that he was
searching for. Then he was invited to attend a worship service at Abyssinian Baptist Church in Harlem, where he sat
under the preaching of Adam Clayton Powell Sr. and experienced a community born of suffering. It was there that
he came to understand that Jesus was more than an intellectual concept—he is actual reality that we can encounter
especially among the oppressed, suffering, and downtrodden.
In Harlem, Bonhoeffer encountered the "lived experience of
Jesus' cross for black people in America."[6] Living, worshiping, and serving with the least of these in America led him
to find solidarity with the least of these back in his home
country of Germany.

Bonhoeffer's *Cost of Discipleship* is first and foremost a
call to embrace the cross. This is seen clearly in what may
be his most well-known quote: "When Christ calls a man,
he bids him come and die."[7] This comes in a section where
Bonhoeffer is trying to prepare us for the moment when
Jesus gives us our cross. Bonhoeffer believed that Jesus lays a
cross on every Christian at the beginning of our relationship
with him. Thus, we need to be prepared for that moment of
bidding.

In fact every command of Jesus is a call to die, with all our affections and lusts. But we do not want to die, and therefore Jesus Christ and his call are necessarily our death as well as our life. The call to discipleship, the baptism in the name of Jesus Christ means both death and life.[8]

The command to baptize people is a command to prepare them for the reality of the cross.

It is worth noting that we have a clearer understanding as to what this means than the original disciples did. When Jesus told them that they must take their cross and follow him, they knew what "a" cross was, but they were yet to learn about "the" cross. Living under Roman rule, they had a general understanding of crucifixion, for they saw the horror of this form of execution on a regular basis. But they did not know what we know. What is past tense for us was still future tense for them. What they would have struggled to understand, we see clearly—God died on the cross and now calls us to follow his example.

Baptism breaks the illusion that the cross was just for Jesus. In my book *Living Sacrifice*, I endeavored to show that Jesus—in his death—was showing us how to live. Peter made it clear that "you were called, because Christ suffered for you, leaving you an example, that you should follow in his steps" (1 Peter 2:21). Jesus' death on the cross is a template for us to pattern our lives after. Jesus' sacrifice on the cross is the blueprint for us to study as we endeavor to offer our bodies as living sacrifices (Romans 12:1). As a matter of fact, all that Jesus did on the cross, we are called to do, albeit imperfectly, as Christ's disciples. Simply put, it's a pain-absorbing, price-paying, peace-making, cup-drinking, and winning-by-losing existence.[9]

The reason we should make the connection between baptism and the cross is that people deserve to know the full truth about a relationship with Jesus so they, too, can count the cost of following him (Luke 14:27-33). In baptism, we give people an opportunity to do so. This is why much of our preaching and one-on-one mentoring needs to focus on helping people understand the implications of the cross upon their relationships, personal conduct, and finances as well helping people see the cost of non-discipleship. French theologian and priest François Fénelon put it this way:

> God prepares a cross for you that you must embrace without thought of self-preservation. The cross is painful. . . . Let me warn you that if you push the cross away, your circumstances will become twice as hard to bear. In the long run, the pain of resisting the cross is harder to live with than the cross itself.[10]

Something special happens when God's people embrace the cross as a lived reality. For example, on May 4, 2015, a group of so-called First-Amendment defenders in Garland, Texas, decided to hold a cartoon "drawing contest" of the prophet Muhammad. The organizers received more than three hundred entries. Muslims believe that such caricatures are blasphemous. In response, two self-avowed ISIS supporters from Phoenix drove to the event with the intent to do harm. They were shot and killed as they opened fire on the gathering.

Since the two gunmen were from Phoenix, a second "contest" was organized there. The "Freedom of Speech Rally Round II" was to take place outside the Islamic Community Center of Phoenix. Attendees wore shirts with vulgar insults directed toward Muslims, burned Qurans, harassed Muslims as they sought to pray, and exercised their Second-Amendment rights by coming to the event fully armed. Tensions were high.

In addition to the many police officers who were there to keep the peace, hundreds of Christians from various churches held their own "Love Your Neighbor Rally" in order to demonstrate the "sacrificial love of Christ by creating a human shield in front of the Mosque."[11]

Pastor Jim Mullins, one of the cross-formed organizers, said,

> Our strategy was to arrive early so that we could fill
> the sidewalk in front of the Mosque, thus forcing the
> hostile protestors to the other side of the street. Also,
> our bodies became a physical barrier of protection
> between the masked men with guns (a lot of guns)
> and our Muslim friends. We wanted to demonstrate
> the pattern of the cross. . . . This is what Jesus did

for us when he was crushed on the cross for sinners like you and me, Muslims at the Mosque, bikers with guns, those watching the events on TV, and the whole world (John 3:16). The cross not only made a way for us to know God, but it's also the path we must walk in this world as his disciples. . . . Therefore, we resolved that if someone opened fire at the Mosque, and upon our Muslim neighbors, the bullets would have to go through us first.

Remarkable! The cross led Christians to love all of their neighbors in a very hostile environment. When all was said and done, not one shot was fired, some of the protesters turned their obscene T-shirts inside out, and Christ was glorified. It was a powerful witness to the world as to what it means to love our neighbor as ourselves. That is the power of the cross lived in and through followers of Jesus. That is why Jesus wants us to prepare people for the cross through baptism.

Teach: Prepared to Love

The second thing Jesus tells us to do as we lead people to him is to "[teach] them to obey everything I have commanded" (Matthew 28:20). This is fascinating. Why would Jesus want us to focus primarily on teaching everything he *commanded*? It's all about loving God the way *he* desires to be loved.

Jesus could have told us to teach people to obey everything he *taught* but instead he singled out a specific slice of

his teaching when he said "everything I have commanded."
Of course, Jesus wants us to know everything he taught, but
he specifically asks us—as we prepare people to be discipled
by him—to make sure they have intimate knowledge of his
commands. This is more than a matter of semantics.

A few years ago, it dawned on me that I had not personally identified all of the commands of Christ. As a teacher
of God's Word, you would have thought I had done so,
given the fact that Jesus made it clear that I am to focus my
teaching largely, though not necessarily exclusively, on his
commands. So I decided to read through the four Gospels,
Acts, a few of the letters of Paul, and the book of Revelation.
Basically, I looked for all the red letters of the Bible in my
search for every single command of Jesus. For five months,
I read, underlined, typed up, and categorized all the commands of Christ I could find. I knew that an Internet search
would have led me to others who had already done the
same, but I wanted the experience of discovering them for
myself. I wanted to wrestle with what was a command only
for the original hearers and which ones were universal for
all of God's people. In many cases, it wasn't clear-cut, but in
the end, I had a dozen or so pages to explore. This exercise
changed my life. Having a categorized list of what Jesus was
actually asking me to teach was invaluable as a pastor, but
even more so as a practicing Christian.[12]

Here's what I discovered: The commands of Christ are
less than 25 percent of all the teachings of Jesus. That's all.

Why would Jesus ask us to focus on such a small percentage

of his teaching as we enroll people in school with him? What it comes down to is this: *Obedience is the love language of Jesus.*

Four times in his upper room discourse, Jesus talked about the relationship between loving and obeying him.

- "If you love me, keep my commands" (John 14:15).
- "Whoever has my commands and keeps them is the one who loves me. The one who loves me will be loved by my Father, and I too will love them and show myself to them" (John 14:21).
- "If you keep my commands, you will remain in my love, just as I have kept my Father's commands and remain in his love" (John 15:10).
- "You are my friends if you do what I command." (John 15:14).

Jesus is telling us that keeping his commands is the foundation of a love-based relationship with him. There is a direct link to loving Jesus and obeying his commands. I don't think it was a coincidence that the "disciple whom Jesus loved" was the one who preserved these passages for us so that we can know specifically how to love Christ in return.[13] Nor was it happenstance that Jesus asked Peter three times "Do you love me?" and then gave him the command to take care of and feed his sheep (John 21:15-19). Three times Peter denied him, so three times Jesus gave Peter a chance to love again by keeping his commands. In the great co-mission, Jesus is asking us to help people understand this so when they begin a discipleship relationship with him, it is based not only on the fact that Jesus loves them and demonstrated it but they also can love him back in a demonstrative way.

Jesus is asking, "Will you teach people to turn the other cheek and to forgive seventy times seven? Will you teach people to store up for themselves treasure in heaven, where moth and rust do not destroy? Will you practically show people how to keep watch, seek first the Kingdom, and not be afraid, because when they do these things, I experience them as love?" When we do as he commands, Jesus will feel loved.

Jesus is looking for more than mere intellectual assent to doctrine. He loves to be loved and desires to be desired, amazingly, by us! This makes sense, given the true nature of what it means to be human. James K. A. Smith, in his book *You Are What You Love*, says that we are "first and foremost *lovers*"[14] and that fundamental fact should affect the way we approach spiritual growth. Smith says that discipleship is about the way we "curate" our hearts because it's "more a matter of hungering and thirsting than of knowing and believing. Jesus' command to follow him is a command to align our loves and longings with his—to want what God wants, to desire what God desires, to hunger and thirst after God and crave a world where he is all in all."[15]

Smith's point is that we have too long thought that we humans are first and foremost thinking beings. That explains why we've approached discipleship cognitively; many times, giving the impression that being a Christian is all about thinking the right things. Jesus highlights what discipleship is really about by asking us to teach people "all that I have commanded." Our minds are important, but our hearts may be even more so.

Leading people in such a way that they obey the commands of Jesus results in the fulfillment of an awe-inspiring promise in their lives. Jesus said, "Whoever has my commands and keeps them is the one who loves me. The one who loves me will be loved by my Father, and I too will love them and show myself to them" (John 14:21).

When we are lovingly obedient, not only does Jesus promise to reciprocate our love but also he says that he will "show myself to them." The result of enrolling people in school with the master disciple maker and ensuring the prerequisite of "obeying everything I have commanded" is that they will have a genuine encounter with Jesus himself!

This is not to say that Jesus' love is conditional or contingent; rather, it is a recognition that our hearts matter when it comes to experiencing the presence of Christ. Jesus promises that he *will* reveal himself to them and to us. The promise is that we will have a one-on-one, firsthand encounter with our risen rabbi. He will know that we are ready for him to disciple us when he sees that our hearts are turned toward him.

We've covered a lot of ground. We've seen that to be discipled by Jesus involves seeing him as our pastor, choosing him as our teacher, and joining him in the great co-mission. We are prepared for this red-letter reality through baptism as we embrace the cross as a way of life and through grace-fueled obedience to the commands of Jesus as we learn to love him. Now we turn our attention to the end goal of discipleship. What does Jesus have in store for the discipled?

CHAPTER EIGHT

THE ULTIMATE GOAL
of Discipleship

The original twelve disciples spent less than three years with Jesus, and then he released them to turn their world upside down. They were ready! And if you've walked with Jesus for a significant amount of time, then you're ready too. Discipleship is *not* the end goal of the Christian life. Jesus disciples us for a reason.

In the church, we have a way of putting people on a perpetual discipleship treadmill. In addition to not making it clear that everyone can be discipled by Jesus (just like the original Twelve) we also lead people to believe that they need to be part of the church's discipleship programs with no apparent end in sight. No graduation. No diploma. Just a lifetime of learning while sitting in pews and folding chairs. The end result is Christians who understand the essentials of the faith but who have missed out on the purpose of all of that training.

I love the church. I believe in it so much that I have given my life to it, but I'm in full agreement with Daniel Taylor, who wrote, "No institution has accomplished so much for good in this world; none has fallen so short of its calling!"[1] All Jesus needed was three years to prepare his disciples to face a hostile world and to stand strong for their King and his Kingdom. Three years and they were ready to plant churches, proclaim the gospel, defend against heresy, and—if necessary—give their lives in the process. *The end goal of discipleship is to be transformed by Jesus for the sake of others.*

What about you? How long have you been a Christian? Are *you* ready? Our family, friends, and neighbors need us to be. If you look around, you'll discover that many have built their lives upon the L.I.E.

L.I.E. is an acronym I use to describe life outside the Kingdom of God: Lost. Isolated. Empty.

- *Lost*: Jesus told us that when we try to find our own way in this world, we end up stuck between the couch cushions like loose change; wedged in dead-end ravines like helpless sheep; or hopeless in pigpens of our own making, like the lost son (Luke 15).

- *Isolated*: In this world divided by race, class, and culture, fear drives us into hiding instead of into genuine love of our neighbors and the reconciling work of Jesus on the cross (Ephesians 2:14-18).

- *Empty*: Os Guinness said it well: "We have too much to live with and too little to live for."[2]

People are in desperate need of the truths that transform the L.I.E. of their life. Christ, Community, and Calling are the life-giving serum.

- It is *Christ* who came to seek and to save that which was *lost* (Luke 19:10).
- Jesus summons the *isolated* to live shame-free in the *community* known as God's family (Romans 8:14-17).
- The *empty* are satiated through the *call* of Christ to pick up our towel and basin and serve (John 13:1-17).

Our neighbors need us to be ready! You've most likely known Jesus for long enough. Jesus will continue to disciple you, but he's doing so for a reason. You are ready to turn your world upside down.

Have you ever done the math? If you've faithfully attended church services for three years, you've heard more than 150 sermons! Additionally, you've had pastors available to answer your questions and most likely availed yourself of classes on how to share your faith and what it means to have godly finances and relationships. You've had time to read most, if not all, of your Bible, and while you may not be an expert, you are well aware of quintessential passages like the Ten Commandments, the Sermon on the Mount, and John 3:16. If someone asked you about Jesus, you could probably walk them through his claim to be God, the virgin birth, his miracles and message of the Kingdom, and his death and resurrection. If you've chosen to be a part of a healthy, life-giving church, then you've experienced his grace and are learning to rest in his mercy. You volunteer and give of your money because you know Jesus is building his church, "and the gates of Hades will not overcome it" (Matthew 16:18). You pray—yes, you may struggle with it—but you pray to your Father in heaven, hallowed be his name. You are ready!

If, after all of this, you don't feel poised for the task, the good news is that *Jesus* is ready. You can ask him to continue to bring you up to speed. Jesus is ready, willing, and able to disciple you himself. But remember: Discipleship is *not* the goal of the Christian life. No, the purpose of discipleship is to prepare us to do the "good works" that God "prepared in advance for us to do" (Ephesians 2:10). Jesus disciples us so we can join him in the great co-mission as we go with him into all of the world.

Those whom Jesus disciples, he sends. This may be why many Christians experience a spiritual crisis after walking with Jesus in intimate, one-on-one fellowship. Perhaps you've experienced a time of doubt and a feeling of distance in your relationship with God. What could be happening during these times is that Jesus, like a parent who has prepared their child to make good decisions and live responsibly, is telling you that you have had enough preparation. It's now time for you to go. That's exactly what happened with the Twelve. After spending every waking hour in school with Jesus as their rabbi, the time came for class to end and their Kingdom mission to begin.

That feeling of distance that we sometimes feel in our relationship could mean that we, too, are in the process of being sent by Jesus. We learn more about the sending aspects of discipleship as we observe the Spirit of Christ at work in the life of Philip.

A Tale of Two Philips

Philip was discipled by Jesus himself. That means he was . . .

- called by Jesus: "The next day Jesus decided to leave for Galilee. Finding Philip, he said to him, 'Follow me'" (John 1:43).
- led by Jesus: "One of those days Jesus went out to a mountainside to pray, and spent the night praying to God. When morning came, he called his disciples to him and chose twelve of them, whom he also designated apostles: Simon (whom he named Peter), his brother Andrew, James, John, *Philip* . . ." (Luke 6:12-14, emphasis added).
- taught by Jesus: "When Jesus looked up and saw a great crowd coming toward him, he said to Philip,

'Where shall we buy bread for these people to eat?'
He asked this only to test him, for he already had in
mind what he was going to do" (John 6:5-6).

- filled by Jesus: "When they arrived, they went
  upstairs to the room where they were staying. Those
  present were Peter, John, James and Andrew; Philip"
  (Acts 1:13). "When the day of Pentecost came, they
  were all together in one place. Suddenly a sound like
  the blowing of a violent wind came from heaven
  and filled the whole house where they were sitting.
  They saw what seemed to be tongues of fire that
  separated and came to rest on each of them. All of
  them were filled with the Holy Spirit and began to
  speak in other tongues as the Spirit enabled them"
  (Acts 2:1-4).

Confession. I had been reading the Bible for most of my
life. I even had an undergraduate degree in biblical studies
and a degree from seminary. Additionally, I had been teaching the Scriptures for at least a decade before I realized that
the Philip above is not the Philip we find in this passage
below.

Those who had been scattered preached the word
wherever they went. Philip went down to a city
in Samaria and proclaimed the Messiah there.
When the crowds heard Philip and saw the signs he
performed, they all paid close attention to what he

said. For with shrieks, impure spirits came out of
many, and many who were paralyzed or lame were
healed. So there was great joy in that city.

ACTS 8:4-8

I had always assumed they were one and the same. I found
out I was in good company because throughout church history these two Philips have often been confused. It's understandable, because the Philip here in Acts 8 was doing
amazing things. He was performing signs and wonders and
affecting the ethos of a whole city through his teaching, so it
is only natural to think that he was one of the original disciples. But there were two Philips.

This Philip in Acts 8 is not the same one who witnessed
the feeding of the five thousand. He's not the Philip who
was present in the upper room when Jesus sent the Holy
Spirit. This Philip was not one of the *Twelve*, he was one of
the *seven*.

In those days when the number of disciples was
increasing, the Hellenistic Jews among them
complained against the Hebraic Jews because
their widows were being overlooked in the daily
distribution of food. So the Twelve gathered all the
disciples together and said, 'It would not be right
for us to neglect the ministry of the word of God
in order to wait on tables. Brothers and sisters,
choose seven men from among you who are known

> to be full of the Spirit and wisdom. We will turn
> this responsibility over to them and will give our
> attention to prayer and the ministry of the word.'
>   This proposal pleased the whole group. They
> chose Stephen, a man full of faith and of the Holy
> Spirit; also *Philip* . . .
>
> ACTS 6:1-5, EMPHASIS ADDED

The church is supposed to care for orphans and widows
in their distress (James 1:27). However, word had reached
the Twelve that something had gone awry and some of the
widows were being overlooked. Knowing that they needed
to give their attention to prayer and teaching the Word, *the
Twelve* set aside *the seven* and handed the ministry over to
them. "They chose Stephen, a man full of faith and of the
Holy Spirit; also Philip" (Acts 6:5).

Philip #1 was the Philip who was part of the Twelve, and
Philip #2 was part of this spirit-filled group of seven. Two
different men who not only shared the same name but also
the same experience of being discipled by the master disciple
maker. What we see with both of them is that part of being
discipled by Jesus is that we need to be prepared for when
Jesus sends us out on Kingdom assignments.

In addition to the great co-mission, Jesus often sent the
Twelve out on short-term trips so they could get used to living life on mission (Matthew 10:1-42; Matthew 28:16-20;
Luke 10:1-24). But you didn't have to be one of the Twelve to
receive a commissioning from Jesus. Attendance at the feeding

of the five thousand or witnessing the Resurrection was not a prerequisite. What Jesus made available to the twelve disciples was experienced by many others, including Philip #2.

This second Philip wasn't there for all of those great moments, yet he, too, was called, led, taught, and filled by Jesus. On this last aspect, Philip #2 gives us needed insight, for Jesus is still sending his people into all the world.

You're a Godsend

In English, we slur words and, over time, create new ones. *You all* became *y'all* and *Christ's Mass* became *Christmas*. The same thing happened with the Old English phrase *Godes sonde*. It was a way of describing that which comes from God. Today, instead of saying *godes sonde*, we say *godsend*. When we are discipled by Jesus, that is exactly what we become: a godsend. That which arrives in people's lives signed, sealed, and delivered from their Savior, Lord, and friend.

Jesus was a godsend.

> For God so loved the world that he gave his one
> and only Son, that whoever believes in him shall
> not perish but have eternal life. For God did not
> send his Son into the world to condemn the world,
> but to save the world through him.
> JOHN 3:16-17

There are a lot of words we use to describe Jesus: loving, kind, divine, human, teacher, Messiah. Jesus liked the word *sent* as a description of his life. God sent his Son, and this "sentness" defined Jesus' mission.

- "'My food,' said Jesus, 'is to do the will of him who sent me and to finish his work'" (John 4:34).
- "By myself I can do nothing; I judge only as I hear, and my judgment is just, for I seek not to please myself but him who sent me" (John 5:30).
- "I have come down from heaven not to do my will but to do the will of him who sent me. And this is the will of him who sent me, that I shall lose none of all those he has given me, but raise them up at the last day" (John 6:38-39).
- "I have much to say in judgment of you. But he who sent me is trustworthy, and what I have heard from him I tell the world" (John 8:26).
- "As long as it is day, we must do the works of him who sent me" (John 9:4).
- "They took away the stone. Then Jesus looked up and said, 'Father, I thank you that you have heard me. I knew that you always hear me, but I said this for the benefit of the people standing here, that they may believe that you sent me'" (John 11:41-42).

Jesus lived a God-sent life. Daily, he was aware of the fact that his Father had commissioned him to speak, act, and love on his behalf. He said that he came to "finish his work" (John 4:34) and not to speak his own words but the words of his Father (John 12:49). Jesus lived dispatched like an ambulance driver headed to the scene of an accident; like a courier with a message to deliver. *Sent* defined Jesus.

To say that Jesus was a godsend is to recognize that his birth, life, teaching, death, and resurrection were commissioned by his Father and that he lived to accomplish that which he was sent to do. As Jesus prayed, "Now my soul is troubled, and what shall I say? 'Father, save me from this hour'? No, it was for this very reason I came to this hour" (John 12:27).

God sent Jesus, so Jesus sends us. Knowing that we have been sent by Jesus gives confidence, assurance, and purpose to everyday life. Living *sent* changes the way we see our circumstances, whether they be a new job, the DMV waiting area, or a change in class at school. We are always on call for our King. The Father sent the Son; the Son sends his disciples.

Living *sent* means that we have been discipled by Jesus and that we are now ready to live as Jesus would live in the world. After Jesus spent three years teaching and training the Twelve, he said to them, "Peace be with you! As the Father has sent me, I am sending you" (John 20:21). The Father sent the Son to serve, heal, feed, forgive, and redeem. The Son sends us out to do the same. This is why the twelve disciples are also known as the twelve apostles—"apostle" literally means one "sent with a message." As his disciples, we, too, become apostles—godsends to the world!

Margaret Clarkson was a schoolteacher in northern

Ontario. Jobs were scarce when she became a certified teacher in 1935, so she spent seven years educating students in gold mining and lumber camps. Feeling isolated and insignificant, she began meditating upon those words of Jesus—"So send I you" (John 20:21, KJV)—and she sensed Jesus telling her that she was every bit a missionary as her friends who were serving overseas in far-off countries. She then wrote that classic missionary hymn "So Send I You."

So send I you—to labor unrewarded,
To serve unpaid, unloved, unsought, unknown,
To bear rebuke, to suffer scorn and scoffing—
So send I you, to toil for Me alone.

So send I you—to bind the bruised and broken,
O'er wand'ring souls to work, to weep, to wake,
To bear the burdens of a world aweary—
So send I you, to suffer for My sake.

So send I you—to loneliness and longing,
With heart ahung'ring for the loved and known,
Forsaking home and kindred, friend and dear one—
So send I you, to know My love alone.

So send I you—to leave your life's ambition,
To die to dear desire, self-will resign,
To labor long, and love where men revile you—
So send I you, to lose your life in Mine.

So send I you—to hearts made hard by hatred,
To eyes made blind because they will not see,
To spend, tho it be blood, to spend and spare not—
So send I you, to taste of Calvary.

"As the Father hath sent Me,
So send I you."[3]

I love how the last stanza ends by turning our attention to Jesus and his cross. Margaret's words describe us all, for Jesus is still handing out assignments on a daily basis.

Two Questions for the Discipled

There are two essential questions for living the sent life, and we want to ask them of Jesus regularly in prayer.

Question #1: "Jesus, where do you want me to go?"

All of Jesus' disciples are missionaries. God has a call and mission for every single one of us, and church is at its best when it's designed and structured for people to discover the answer to this question.

This question helps us to see that church isn't the place where we go to be discipled (because Jesus is the master disciple maker), but rather it's the place where the discipled gather as they are living the sent life. Our local church becomes a *base camp*. It's the place where we find rest, inspiration, equipping, and first aid for our souls—all for the purpose of preparing us for the mission that Jesus has for us. Church is a launching pad for what God is doing in your life, a missionary-sending agency. When church assumes that Jesus is speaking to everyone—calling, teaching, filling, and sending—then it seeks to fan the flames of what God is doing in people's lives.

This is why I think that every Christian should have a passport. It's a statement of faith. When we get a passport, we are surrendering to the end goal of discipleship, namely, that Jesus intends to send us to the nations. A passport is a declaration to God that we are ready to go.

At Colorado Community Church, anytime someone gets out of the pew and onto a plane for the cause of Christ, we put a flag on the wall representing the country Jesus sent them to. Dozens of flags decorate our sanctuary, regularly reminding us that the ultimate goal of our gathering is to live sent by Jesus. Church doesn't begin until the worship service ends. Church is what happens when we get out of the seats and into the streets.

Having a passport is a way of saying, "Jesus, I'm ready. I recognized that I am one of your sent ones, and I am prepared to go wherever you want me to go." It's a tangible way of declaring to God that we will cross borders for him. A willingness to cross an ocean also displays a heart that is open to driving across town or walking across the street, for the nations are at our doorstep. Like Margaret Clarkson, we begin to see our current circumstances as a mission field that God has sent us to.

Question #2: "Jesus, why am I here?"

This question recognizes that God is sovereignly at work in our lives. If Jesus is sending, then we can assume that where we are right now is a divine appointment. As Paul said, "He determined the times set for [us] and the exact places where [we] should live" (Acts 17:26).[4] Your birth was God's first divine directive, for at that moment God was sending you into a family. Your childhood street address was not an accident.

How does that change your perspective on the events of your life? Did your father's employer send your family around the country, or was it Jesus? What about your adoption? As tragic as it was for you not to grow up with your birth family, are you open to the possibility that Jesus was with you? This is why it's important for us to ask Jesus, "Why am I here?"

My wife, Barbara, needed to take a quick trip to the grocery store. After shopping, she chose a checkout lane with only one person in line . . . only to realize that there was a rather involved conversation taking place between the cashier and that customer in front of her. While she was tempted to switch lines for the sake of time, she paused and opened herself to the possibility that Jesus wanted her in that line. Prayerfully, she tuned in to what was taking place in her presence.

The customer had more groceries than money and was in the process of prioritizing what she could do without. The decisions were not clear, as she only had $60 in her purse but had rung up $150 in groceries. "How much is that?" the woman asked again and again, and Barbara quickly realized the mission that Jesus had sent her on. She discreetly covered the woman's deficit. When my wife reached the cashier, he apologized for the delay. Barbara replied, "No apology needed. God sent me here for this very reason."

Life with Jesus is an adventure. Every day is a potential Kingdom assignment. Wherever you and I are or are going is full of purpose and potential. We see this in the life of Philip #2.

The early church was under attack. Followers of Jesus were being stoned to death in the streets, and "all except the apostles were scattered throughout Judea and Samaria" (Acts 8:1). That's how Philip ended up in Samaria. This disruption in his life turned him into a godsend for many people as he preached the gospel and performed miracles, alleviating the suffering of many (Acts 8:4-8). He wasn't just running for his life, he was going were Jesus was sending him. That's when he encountered the angel with a message from Jesus himself.

Now an angel of the Lord said to Philip, "Go south to the road—the desert road—that goes down from Jerusalem to Gaza." So he started out, and on his way he met an Ethiopian eunuch, an important official in charge of all the treasury of the Kandake (which means "queen of the Ethiopians"). This man had gone to Jerusalem to worship, and on his way home was sitting in his chariot reading the Book of Isaiah the prophet. The Spirit told Philip, "Go to that chariot and stay near it."

ACTS 8:26-29

There was a man who deeply desired to worship and was trying to figure out his relationship with God. This Ethiopian eunuch was actually reading about Jesus when Jesus sent Philip to him to tell him about Jesus! The Ethiopian official gave his life to Christ on the spot, was baptized by Philip, and then took the gospel into the heart of Africa.

Philip lived *sent*. What about you? Do you know that you are a godsend? Do you have your passport?

God's Plans for Y'all

We take the *sent* life to the next level by restating the two essential questions in the plural.

"God, why am *I* here?" becomes "God, why are *we* here?"

"God, where do you want *me* to go?" becomes "God, where do you want *us* to go?"

God also works with groups of people. In the Old Testament, God sent all of Israel as a light to the nations (Isaiah 49:6). In the New Testament, Jesus sent his disciples out two by two (Mark 6:7; Luke 10:1). Jesus' sending activity isn't just about "me" but "we," which alters every relationship we find ourselves in.

If you're married, this means that you are covenanted for

life with your spouse because Jesus has joined you together for a Kingdom reason. You are stronger together than you could ever be apart, and God's calling is for both of you.

Next time you're worshiping with your church, look around and ask, "Jesus, why are *we* here? Jesus, where do you want *us* to go?" You'll begin to see church not just as a missionary-sending agency but as a collective missionary endeavor that Jesus has sent to your town or city.

Most people go to Jeremiah 29 because of verse 11: "'For I know the plans I have for you,' declares the LORD, 'plans to prosper you and not to harm you, plans to give you hope and a future.'" We love that verse because it gives hope for our individual lives. While it's true that God knit each of us together in the womb (Psalm 139:13) and knows the number of hairs on our heads (Matthew 10:30), this verse is about so much more. In the original language, it's not singular but *plural*. It reads more like this: "'I know the plans I have for [y'all],' declares the LORD, 'plans to prosper [y'all] and not to harm [y'all].'" He's talking to a group of people he had sent on a mission together. Groups of people can struggle with and forget their purpose, just like individuals.

In Jeremiah 29, God is reminding his people of the reasons he sent them to Babylon. They thought they were prisoners of war, and all they wanted was to return home to Jerusalem. So God, through his prophet, sent this letter telling them that they were not there by accident. Yes, he had plans to take them back to Jerusalem eventually, but for the time being, they needed to settle down, build houses, plant crops, and have children, because it was going to be a while—seventy years, in fact (Jeremiah 29:10)!

In the meantime, he had a collective call for his people: "Seek the peace and prosperity of the city to which I have carried you into exile. Pray to the LORD for it, because if it prospers, you too will prosper" (Jeremiah 29:7).

God reframes their situation by saying, "Y'all think you're in Babylon because of the Babylonians? You're not there because of *them*; you're there because of me! I sent y'all there." A whole nation had to change the way they saw themselves. They were together in that place for a reason.

Think again about your home church. Could there be a unique reason God has you all together? What is it about the nation, state, city, or town where it's located?

The church I'm part of knows that God has called us together to break down the barriers of race and class. We dream of the day that 11:00 on Sunday morning is no longer the most segregated hour in America. We are together— Baptist and Presbyterian, Democrat and Republican—so that we might reach the lost, care for the downtrodden, shelter the homeless, feed the hungry, write résumés for the unemployed, provide legal aid for victims of domestic violence, and offer hope to the addict.

While each of us could tackle these things as individuals, we know we'll be more effective if we work together. Together, we do justice, love mercy, and walk humbly with our God (Micah 6:8) when it comes to gendercide around the world or the dignity of immigrants and refugees in our own backyard. Together, God has placed us where we are to wash the feet of the city to which he has carried us.

This collective call also extends beyond our local church. When Jesus looks at our city, he sees one church that happens to meet in fifteen hundred locations. All in the city together for a reason.

After Barbara and I had our first child biologically, we decided to build our family through adoption. In our city, there were many children in need of a forever family, and the Bible says, "Religion that God our Father accepts as pure and faultless is this: to look after orphans and widows in their distress and to keep oneself from being polluted by the world" (James 1:27). The call to care for orphans is for the whole body of Christ—every Christian in every church. There is a myriad of ways for us to live out that calling. For my wife and me, adoption felt most natural, and today we have six children, of whom five are adopted (three from foster care, two from Ethiopia). God desires for the whole bride of Christ to play a role in the lives of children, for he is "father to the fatherless" and "sets the lonely in families" (Psalm 68:5-6). We began to realize that our individual call was also the collective call of the church, for every child deserves a home.

A decade ago, in Colorado, there were almost nine hundred children in our foster care system ready for adoption. Children without parents, waiting for homes. We began to dream . . . *There are fifteen hundred churches in the Denver metro area. If every church took one child, you'd have a waiting list of families, not a waiting list of children!* That was the beginning of Project 1.27, a ministry dedicated to finding a home for every child in Colorado's foster care system. Over the last decade, Project 1.27 has magnified Christ's call to serve the orphan to the community of believers, and we have seen dozens of churches come together in this effort. Thousands of Christians have trained to foster and adopt in faith. What began as a local effort has spread around the country to Seattle, Florida, New York, Arizona, Wisconsin, Kansas, Louisiana, and Washington, DC.

All of this has happened because Christians are living a collective call. Together, they responded to the call of Jesus in the place where he has sent them.[5]

We are where *we* are for a reason.

His Name Was Terry

Terry was a white-haired homeless man who loved hanging out in the parking lot of our church building. Due to a motorcycle accident in his twenties, he moved around slowly, aided by a metal walker. Too proud to accept help, he lived in the field across the street. Every morning he'd cross one of the busiest intersections in our city; with crossing light blinking and horns blaring, he slowly trekked to our side of the street to set up shop for the day.

One day I said, "Hey, Terry, how are you doing?"

He swung around, alcohol on his breath, anger in his eyes, and began shouting—not at me but at God—"Why do you hate me? Why is my life so bad?" Looking to the sky, he said, "I'm a bug to you. A bug! In the same way I squash bugs, you have squashed my life." I could feel his desperation. I wanted to help.

When he sobered up, I asked him if he knew about the most prayed prayer of the Bible—*Lord, have mercy.* He wanted to know more, so I told him that no other sentence was spoken to Jesus more than this simple request. Wonderfully, Jesus responded to this request *every single time.* Not once did Jesus turn away without showing mercy. I told Terry that he, too, could pray this prayer, and he could even do it as he slept in the field at night, praying it in rhythm with his heartbeat. This man who thought God hated him decided to make the most prayed prayer in the Bible the most prayed prayer in his life.

At the time, I was writing my book *The Mercy Prayer,*[6] so I asked Terry if he wanted to be one of my proofreaders, explaining that his perspective could help me and that the subject matter might help him sort through whether or not God was really mad at him. He agreed, and each time I finished a chapter, Terry would correct my grammatical mistakes and write questions in the margins that we'd talk about. This continued until winter, when he went into "hibernation." He had given me his cell phone number, and on especially cold nights, I'd call him to see if he'd found his way indoors. It was hard to keep track of him.

One spring morning, Terry leaned up against our building and died. As a staff, we gathered on the sidewalk, marked the spot with a cross, and thanked God for Terry's life. Why did Terry come to our corner? Why did he battle traffic twice a day when there were plenty of other places to relax and rest? It wasn't just for the liquor store in the strip mall next to our building, because there's another one on the other side of the street too.

Why did he keep coming, season after season, year after year? The best answer I can come up with is *us*—the church. I wasn't the only one who reached out to Terry. No, many of our staff and congregation genuinely loved and cared for him. The night before he died, our youth group slept outside in cardboard boxes to learn how to identify with the homeless. The next morning when they saw Terry, one of them shared a cheese stick with him. Little did he know that he was serving Terry his last meal.

Terry came to that corner because *we* are on that corner. He never attended a service. As far as I know, Terry never set foot in our old, renovated movie-theater building. But he stayed close to us to warm his heart with the love God had for him in us. He was sent to us. We were sent to him.

When no one claimed his body, we contacted the county coroner. "He's one of us. We were/are his family." We picked up his cremated remains and turned all of our services that weekend into a memorial service for Terry, and I eulogized his life in my sermon.

It was a reminder to us all that to be discipled by Jesus is to live a sent life. Jesus intends the church to be a godsend to its community. Together, *we* as God's people are sent—knowingly and unknowingly—as instruments of mercy and grace. We are not where we are by accident; everywhere is a divine appointment.

To this day, Terry's urn sits in my office.

EPILOGUE

The Thirteenth Disciple

——— + ———

I love the work of John August Swanson.[1] He's an American painter whose art reflects the eclectic heritage he inherited from a Mexican mother and a Swedish father. He tells biblical stories using vivid imagery—oftentimes using upward of eighty colors in a painting. His work is a feast for the eyes.

I find his depiction of Jesus washing the disciples' feet most intriguing of all of Swanson's work. Using a serigraph process with thirty layers of color, Swanson displays four miniature scenes across the top of the painting: Jesus and the woman at the well; Jesus and the children; Mary Magdalene anointing Jesus; and the parable of the Good Samaritan. In the foreground, we see Jesus in the upper room with his disciples. They surround him as he kneels and washes the feet of the disciple seated in front of him. If you get a chance to see this masterpiece, be sure to take some time and count the number of disciples in the room with Jesus. There aren't twelve disciples but *thirteen*.

Who is this thirteenth disciple? I like to think that it could be me. It could be you!

That's the promise of spiritual growth in light of the Resurrection. As Luke Timothy Johnson points out, "The 'Jesus movement' ended with Jesus' death, but it started up again after his resurrection."[2] Because Jesus is alive, we all can experience Jesus in ways similar to the original Twelve. We can be that thirteenth disciple.

So do you want to know why Jesus would reach out to you like he did Ananias?

There's only one way to discover your role in the great co-mission. If you're wondering *Why me?*, the answer to that question (and many more) can only be found at the feet of Jesus. Let Jesus himself call, teach, fill, and send you. For Jesus always has been and always will be the master disciple maker!

He is risen! He is risen indeed!

APPENDIX A

A Personal Guide to Loving Jesus

—— ✝ ——

The commands of Christ play a special role in our relationship with Jesus. Namely, they teach us how to love him. For Jesus said, "If you love me, keep my commands" (John 14:15).

I encourage you to discover them for yourself. Read through the Gospels, Acts, and Revelation in search of the commands of Jesus. In this appendix, I provide my personal compilation as an example of what you might create.

Don't get caught up in perfectionism. You'll no doubt find inconsistencies and omissions in my list. There are some commands that are clear and universal. Others are specific to the situation that Jesus was addressing but are still applicable to all people. Others are exclusively unique to the setting and not meant for us (i.e., when Jesus commands non-people such as demons or nature).

As you undertake this study, prayerfully ask Jesus to teach you how to love him.

Awareness

- "Watch out for false prophets" (Matthew 7:15).
- "Watch out that no one deceives you" (Matthew 24:4).
- "Keep watch, because you do not know on what day your Lord will come" (Matthew 24:42).
- "Understand this: If the owner of the house had known at what time of night the thief was coming, he would have kept watch and would not have let his house be broken into" (Matthew 24:43).
- "Keep watch, because you do not know the day or the hour" (Matthew 25:13).
- "Watch and pray so that you will not fall into temptation. The spirit is willing, but the flesh is weak" (Matthew 26:41).
- "Watch out for the teachers of the law" (Mark 12:38).
- "Watch out that no one deceives you" (Mark 13:5).
- "You must be on your guard" (Mark 13:9).
- "Be on your guard; I have told you everything ahead of time" (Mark 13:23).
- "Be on guard! Be alert!" (Mark 13:33).
- "Keep watch because you do not know when the owner of the house will come back. . . . What I say to you, I say to everyone: 'Watch!'" (Mark 13:35-36).
- "Stay here and keep watch" (Mark 14:34).
- "Watch and pray so that you will not fall into temptation. The spirit is willing, but the flesh is weak" (Mark 14:38).

- "Watch out! Be on your guard against all kinds of greed; life does not consist in an abundance of possessions" (Luke 12:15).
- "Watch out that you are not deceived. For many will come in my name, claiming, 'I am he,' and, 'The time is near.' Do not follow them" (Luke 21:8).
- "Be always on the watch, and pray that you may be able to escape all that is about to happen" (Luke 21:36).
- "Pray that you will not fall into temptation" (Luke 22:40).
- "Get up and pray so that you will not fall into temptation" (Luke 22:46).
- "Wake up!" (Revelation 3:2).
- "Look, I come like a thief!" (Revelation 16:15).
- "Look, I am coming soon!" (Revelation 22:7).
- "Look, I am coming soon!" (Revelation 22:12).

Be Careful

- "Be careful not to practice your righteousness in front of others to be seen by them" (Matthew 6:1).

Be Like Your Heavenly Father

- "Be perfect, therefore, as your heavenly Father is perfect" (Matthew 5:48).
- "Be merciful, just as your Father is merciful" (Luke 6:36).

Belief and Faith

- "Have faith in God" (Mark 11:22).
- You believe in God; believe also in me" (John 14:1).
- "Believe me when I say that I am in the Father and the Father is in me; or at least believe on the evidence of the works themselves" (John 14:11).

Children

- "Let the little children come to me, and do not hinder them, for the kingdom of heaven belongs to such as these" (Matthew 19:14).
- "Let the little children come to me, and do not hinder them, for the kingdom of God belongs to such as these" (Luke 18:16).

Fear

- "Do not be afraid of them" (Matthew 10:26).
- "Do not be afraid of those who kill the body but cannot kill the soul. Rather, be afraid of the One who can destroy both soul and body in hell" (Matthew 10:28).
- "Don't be afraid" (Matthew 10:31).
- "Get up. . . . Don't be afraid. . . . Don't tell anyone what you have seen, until the Son of Man has been raised from the dead" (Matthew 17:7, 9).
- "Do not be afraid. Go and tell my brothers to go to Galilee; there they will see me" (Matthew 28:10).
- "Don't be afraid; just believe" (Mark 5:36).

- "Take courage! It is I. Don't be afraid" (Mark 6:50).
- "Don't be afraid; from now on you will fish for people" (Luke 5:10).
- "Don't be afraid; just believe, and she will be healed" (Luke 8:50).
- "Don't be afraid; you are worth more than many sparrows" (Luke 12:7).
- "Do not be afraid, little flock, for your Father has been pleased to give you the kingdom" (Luke 12:32).
- "Do not be frightened" (Luke 21:9).
- "It is I; don't be afraid" (John 6:20).
- "Do not be afraid. I am the First and the Last" (Revelation 1:17).
- "Do not be afraid of what you are about to suffer" (Revelation 2:10).

Follow

- "Come, follow me . . . and I will send you out to fish for people" (Matthew 4:19).
- "Follow me, and let the dead bury their own dead" (Matthew 8:22).
- "Follow me" (Matthew 9:9; Mark 2:14; Luke 5:27; 9:59; John 1:43; 21:19).
- "Come, follow me . . . and I will send you out to fish for people" (Mark 1:17).
- "Sell everything you have and give to the poor, and you will have treasure in heaven. Then come, follow me" (Luke 18:22).

Forgive

- "Forgive, and you will be forgiven" (Luke 6:37).
- "Watch yourselves. If your brother or sister sins against you, rebuke them; and if they repent, forgive them. Even if they sin against you seven times in a day and seven times come back to you saying 'I repent,' you must forgive them" (Luke 17:3-4).

Holy Spirit

- "Receive the Holy Spirit" (John 20:22).
- "Do not leave Jerusalem, but wait for the gift my Father promised, which you have heard me speak about" (Acts 1:4).

Kingdom

- "Seek first his kingdom and his righteousness, and all these things will be given to you as well" (Matthew 6:33).
- "Enter through the narrow gate" (Matthew 7:13).
- "Seek his kingdom, and these things will be given to you as well" (Luke 12:31).
- "Make every effort to enter through the narrow door, because many, I tell you, will try to enter and will not be able to" (Luke 13:24).

Learn

- "Go and learn what this means: 'I desire mercy, not sacrifice'" (Matthew 9:13).

- "Come to me, all you who are weary and burdened, and I will give you rest. Take my yoke upon you and learn from me" (Matthew 11:28-30).
- "Learn this lesson from the fig tree: As soon as its twigs get tender and its leaves come out, you know that summer is near" (Matthew 24:32).

Let Your Light Shine

- "In the same way, let your light shine before others, that they may see your good deeds and glorify your Father in heaven" (Matthew 5:16).

Let Your Yes Be Yes and Your No Be No

- "Do not swear an oath at all: either by heaven, for it is God's throne; or by the earth, for it is his footstool; or by Jerusalem, for it is the city of the Great King. And do not swear by your head, for you cannot make even one hair white or black. All you need to say is simply 'Yes' or 'No'; anything beyond this comes from the evil one" (Matthew 5:34-37).

Listen and Understand

- "What goes into someone's mouth does not defile them, but what comes out of their mouth, that is what defiles them" (Matthew 15:11).
- "Listen to me, everyone, and understand this. Nothing outside a person can defile them by going

into them. Rather, it is what comes out of a person
that defiles them" (Mark 7:14-15).

- "Listen carefully to what I am about to tell you: The
  Son of Man is going to be delivered into the hands of
  men" (Luke 9:44).
- "Listen to what the unjust judge says. And will not
  God bring about justice for his chosen ones, who cry
  out to him day and night?" (Luke 18:6-7).

Mission with God

- "As you go, proclaim this message: 'The kingdom
  of heaven has come near'" (Matthew 10:7).
- "Let both grow together until the harvest"
  (Matthew 13:30).
- "Go and make disciples of all nations, baptizing them
  in the name of the Father and of the Son and of the
  Holy Spirit, and teaching them to obey everything I
  have commanded you" (Matthew 28:19-20).
- "Return home and tell how much God has done
  for you" (Luke 8:39).
- "Let the dead bury their own dead, but you go
  and proclaim the kingdom of God" (Luke 9:60).

Money and Possessions

- "Do not store up for yourselves treasures on earth, where
  moths and vermin destroy, and where thieves break in
  and steal. But store up for yourselves treasures in heaven,

where moths and vermin do not destroy, and where thieves do not break in and steal" (Matthew 6:19-20).

- "Give to everyone who asks you, and if anyone takes what belongs to you, do not demand it back" (Luke 6:30).
- "Give, and it will be given to you" (Luke 6:38).

Peace

- "Have salt among yourselves, and be at peace with each other" (Mark 9:50).

Prayer

- "Ask the Lord of the harvest, therefore, to send out workers into his harvest field" (Matthew 9:38; Luke 10:2).
- "When you pray, say . . ." (Luke 11:2).
- "Ask and you will receive, and your joy will be complete" (John 16:24).

Prohibitions

- "Do not think that I have come to abolish the Law or the Prophets" (Matthew 5:17).
- "Do not judge" (Matthew 7:1).
- "Leave them; they are blind guides. If the blind lead the blind, both will fall into a pit" (Matthew 15:14).
- "Do not do what they do, for they do not practice what they preach" (Matthew 23:3).

- "You are not to be called 'Rabbi,' for you have one Teacher, and you are all brothers. And do not call anyone on earth 'father,' for you have one Father, and he is in heaven. Nor are you to be called instructors, for you have one Instructor, the Messiah" (Matthew 23:8-10).
- "At that time if anyone says to you, 'Look, here is the Messiah!' or, 'There he is!' do not believe it" (Matthew 24:23).
- "If anyone tells you, 'There he is, out in the wilderness,' do not go out; or, 'Here he is, in the inner rooms,' do not believe it" (Matthew 24:26).
- "Be careful. . . . Watch out for the yeast of the Pharisees and that of Herod" (Mark 8:15).
- "Watch out for the teachers of the law" (Mark 12:38).
- "Do not condemn, and you will not be condemned" (Luke 6:37).
- "First take the plank out of your eye, and then you will see clearly to remove the speck from your brother's eye" (Luke 6:42).
- "Be on your guard against the yeast of the Pharisees, which is hypocrisy" (Luke 12:1).
- "When someone invites you to a wedding feast, do not take the place of honor" (Luke 14:8).
- "Do not work for food that spoils, but for food that endures to eternal life, which the Son of Man will give you. For on him God the Father has placed his seal of approval" (John 6:27).

- "Stop judging by mere appearances, but instead judge correctly" (John 7:24).
- "Do not believe me unless I do the works of my Father" (John 10:37).
- "Do not let your hearts be troubled" (John 14:1).

Reconciliation

- "If you are offering your gift at the altar and there remember that your brother or sister has something against you, leave your gift there in front of the altar. First go and be reconciled to them; then come and offer your gift" (Matthew 5:23-24).
- "Settle matters quickly with your adversary who is taking you to court. Do it while you are still together on the way" (Matthew 5:25).

Rejoice

- "Rejoice in that day and leap for joy, because great is your reward in heaven" (Luke 6:23).
- "Do not rejoice that the spirits submit to you, but rejoice that your names are written in heaven" (Luke 10:20).

Relationships

- "Be as shrewd as snakes and as innocent as doves" (Matthew 10:16).
- "What God has joined together, let no one separate" (Mark 10:9).

- "Do to others as you would have them do to you" (Luke 6:31).
- "Now that I, your Lord and Teacher, have washed your feet, you also should wash one another's feet" (John 13:14).
- "A new command I give you: Love one another. As I have loved you, so you must love one another. By this everyone will know that you are my disciples, if you love one another" (John 13:34-35).
- "My command is this: Love each other as I have loved you" (John 15:12).
- "This is my command: Love each other" (John 15:17).

Relationships with Authorities

- "Give back to Caesar what is Caesar's, and to God what is God's" (Matthew 22:21).
- "Bring me a denarius and let me look at it. . . . Give back to Caesar what is Caesar's and to God what is God's" (Mark 12:15, 17).
- "Give back to Caesar what is Caesar's, and to God what is God's" (Luke 20:25).

Relationships with Enemies

- "Do not resist an evil person. If anyone slaps you on the right cheek, turn to them the other cheek also. And if anyone wants to sue you and take your shirt, hand over your coat as well. If anyone forces you to go one mile, go with them two miles. Give to the one

who asks you, and do not turn away from the one
who wants to borrow from you" (Matthew 5:39-42).

- "Love your enemies and pray for those who persecute
  you" (Matthew 5:44).
- "Be careful. . . . Be on your guard against the yeast of
  the Pharisees and Sadducees" (Matthew 16:6, 11).
- "Love your enemies, do good to those who hate you,
  bless those who curse you, pray for those who mistreat
  you" (Luke 6:27-28).
- "If someone slaps you on one cheek, turn to them
  the other also" (Luke 6:29).
- "If someone takes your coat, do not withhold your
  shirt from them" (Luke 6:29).
- "Love your enemies, do good to them, and lend
  to them without expecting to get anything back"
  (Luke 6:35).
- "Beware of the teachers of the law" (Luke 20:46).

Relationship with God

- "Love the Lord your God with all your heart and with
  all your soul and with all your mind. . . . Love your
  neighbor as yourself" (Matthew 22:37-39).
- "Hear, O Israel: The Lord our God, the Lord is one.
  Love the Lord your God with all your heart and with
  all your soul and with all your mind and with all
  your strength. . . . Love your neighbor as yourself"
  (Mark 12:29-31).
- "You must be born again" (John 3:7).

- "Remain in me, as I also remain in you" (John 15:4).
- "Remain in my love" (John 15:9).

Relationships with the Poor

- "If you want to be perfect, go, sell your possessions and give to the poor, and you will have treasure in heaven. Then come, follow me" (Matthew 19:21).
- "Go, sell everything you have and give to the poor, and you will have treasure in heaven. Then come, follow me" (Mark 10:21).
- "Sell your possessions and give to the poor" (Luke 12:33).
- "When you give a luncheon or dinner, do not invite your friends, your brothers or sisters, your relatives, or your rich neighbors; . . . when you give a banquet, invite the poor, the crippled, the lame, the blind" (Luke 14:12-13).
- "Sell everything you have and give to the poor, and you will have treasure in heaven. Then come, follow me" (Luke 18:22).

Remember

- "Take and eat; this is my body" (Matthew 26:26).
- "Drink from it, all of you" (Matthew 26:27).
- "Take it; this is my body" (Mark 14:22).
- "Take this and divide it among you. For I tell you I will not drink again from the fruit of the vine until the kingdom of God comes" (Luke 22:17-18).
- "Do this in remembrance of me" (Luke 22:19).

- "Remember what I told you: 'A servant is not greater than his master'" (John 15:20).
- "Remember, therefore, what you have received and heard; hold it fast, and repent" (Revelation 3:3).

Repent

- "Repent, for the kingdom of heaven has come near" (Matthew 4:17).
- "The time has come. . . . The kingdom of God has come near. Repent and believe the good news!" (Mark 1:15).
- "Repent therefore!" (Revelation 2:16).
- "Remember, therefore, what you have received and heard; hold it fast, and repent" (Revelation 3:3).

Sin

- "If your right eye causes you to stumble, gouge it out and throw it away. . . . And if your right hand causes you to stumble, cut it off and throw it away" (Matthew 5:29-30).
- "If your brother or sister sins, go and point out their fault, just between the two of you. . . . But if they will not listen, take one or two others along. . . . If they still refuse to listen, tell it to the church; and if they refuse to listen even to the church, treat them as you would a pagan or a tax collector" (Matthew 18:15-17).

- "If your hand causes you to stumble, cut it off. . . .
And if your foot causes you to stumble, cut it off. . . .
And if your eye causes you to stumble, pluck it out"
(Mark 9:43-47).

Take Heart

- "Take heart, son; your sins are forgiven" (Matthew 9:2).
- "Take heart, daughter . . . your faith has healed you"
(Matthew 9:22).
- "Take heart! I have overcome the world" (John 16:33).

Testimony and Witness

- "Go home to your own people and tell them how
much the Lord has done for you, and how he has
had mercy on you" (Mark 5:19).
- "See to it, then, that the light within you is not
darkness" (Luke 11:35).

Worry

- "I tell you, do not worry about your life, what you
will eat or drink; or about your body, what you will
wear" (Matthew 6:25).
- "Do not worry about tomorrow, for tomorrow will
worry about itself. Each day has enough trouble of its
own" (Matthew 6:34).
- "Do not worry about what to say or how to say it"
(Matthew 10:19).

- "When you are brought before synagogues, rulers and authorities, do not worry about how you will defend yourselves or what you will say, for the Holy Spirit will teach you at that time what you should say" (Luke 12:11-12).
- "I tell you, do not worry about your life, what you will eat; or about your body, what you will wear. For life is more than food, and the body more than clothes. Consider the ravens. . . . Consider how the wild flowers grow" (Luke 12:22-24, 27).

APPENDIX B

How Being with Jesus Changes Us

———— ✝ ————

When they saw . . . that they were unschooled,
ordinary men, they were astonished and they took
note that these men had been with Jesus.
ACTS 4:13

It was noteworthy that the early disciples "had been with" Jesus. Like a baby duck that follows and mimics the first creature it sees after hatching, the disciples had been "imprinted" by Jesus, and they had taken on his characteristics.

In chapter 6, I explained how I set out to discover what those noteworthy characteristics might have been. I read through the New Testament and made two lists of descriptors, one about Jesus and the other about the disciples and the early church. I then compared the two lists looking for overlaps. Five phrases seemed to capture what was noteworthy about those early disciples who had been with Jesus—that is, what was true of Jesus and true of the early church. These five phrases became an "imprint statement" for our church and my life.

Feel free to adopt this imprint statement as your own. However, after undertaking your own study, you'll most likely settle on different words that capture what you discover.

Worship-Driven

Jesus was a worshiper. We see this clearly when Satan offered Jesus everything if he would just "bow down and worship" him. Jesus replied, "Away from me, Satan! For it is written: 'Worship the Lord your God, and serve him only'" (Matthew 4:9-10).

Jesus used two specific words for worship in his response to the tempter: *proskuneo*, which means "to bow down" (literally, "to kiss toward"), and *latreuo*, which means "to serve." For me, the perfect symbol of true worship is the towel and basin Jesus used to wash the feet of his disciples (John 13:1-17). As we serve the practical needs of our neighbors, we bow down in honor of God. This expands our understanding of worship: It's more than a worship service. Literally, worship *is* service.

Following in the footsteps of Jesus, the early disciples were a worshiping community. They embodied Jesus as they gathered for prayer, praise, and the proclamation of the living Word. However, Jesus and the early disciples show us that worship was more than songs they sang (Acts 2:42-47; 4:32-37). Worship is a way of life.

Spirit-Led

Jesus lived in reliance on the Spirit. The Spirit was present at his incarnation (Luke 1:34-35), descended on his baptism (Luke 3:21-22), and empowered his first sermon (Luke 4:18). When Jesus set out to fast for forty days, he was "led by the Spirit into the wilderness" (Matthew 4:1). The literal translation is "Jesus set sail by the Spirit"—the beauty of the Spirit-led life.

Jesus told the early disciples that they, too, were to live a life in response to the Spirit of God (the "wind" of God; John 3:8). In the book of Acts, we see the disciples waiting for and receiving the Spirit (Acts 1–2) and then living with the sails of their souls filled with the Spirit (see, for example, Acts 2:2; 4:8; 6:3-5; 7:55; 9:17; 11:24; 13:9, 52).

Prayer-Dependent

Jesus prayed constantly. During his baptism, we read, "As he was praying, heaven was opened" (Luke 3:21). Jesus prayed early in the morning and "often withdrew to lonely places and prayed" (Luke 5:16; see also Luke 4:42). Before he chose the twelve disciples he "went out to a mountainside to pray, and spent the night praying to God" (Luke 6:12). Jesus lived a prayer-dependent life.

Prayer was an integral part of life for the first disciples. We read that "they all joined together constantly in prayer" (Acts 1:14) and "devoted themselves . . . to prayer" (Acts 2:42). They prayed when threatened, persecuted, or imprisoned (Acts 4:23-24, 31; 12:12). Prayer was a way of life for the early church (Acts 13:3; 16:25; 21:5)—so much so that the goal for the Christian life was—and still is—to "pray without ceasing" (1 Thessalonians 5:17, ESV). For the disciples, the question was not "Did we pray today?" but "Did we ever stop praying today?"

Grace-Centered

God loves you, and there's nothing you can do about it! That's the message of grace. Jesus came to us "full of grace and truth" (John 1:14) and offered that grace freely to the hungry, broken, and marginalized. He gave second chances to those caught in sin and taught us that "my grace is sufficient for you, for my power is made perfect in weakness" (2 Corinthians 12:9; see also Luke 19:1-10 and John 7:53–8:11).

Early disciples were known for their grace. Stephen, for example, was a "man full of God's grace" (Acts 6:8) and demonstrated God's lavish love as he served the hungry. The apostle Paul, after encountering Jesus, became a herald for the incredible grace of God and proclaimed that grace in every one of his letters (see, for example, Ephesians 2:8).

Kingdom-Obsessed

Jesus' number one topic was the Kingdom of God. "The kingdom of God is like" was one of his favorite ways to begin a parable (see, for example, Mark 4:26). Jesus promised the Kingdom and taught the disciples to pray for its arrival. The Kingdom was not *a* message but *the* message of Jesus, for he is "KING OF KINGS AND LORD OF LORDS" (Revelation 19:16). Jesus is, however, a different kind of King: He has a crown, but it's made of thorns. He has a purple robe, but it's soaked in his own blood.

Jesus' number one topic became the primary pursuit of the early church. They were obsessed with the Kingdom because Jesus had told them to "seek first his kingdom" (Matthew 6:33). We observe the disciples arguing and jostling for their spot in the coming Kingdom; when Jesus rose from the dead they asked, "Lord, are you at this time going to restore the kingdom to Israel?" (Acts 1:6). Even the thief on the cross requested, "Jesus, remember me when you come into your kingdom" (Luke 23:42).

The early church defied the Roman Empire by proclaiming, "Jesus is Lord" instead of "Caesar is lord" (Romans 10:9). "Maranatha!" (or "Come, Lord!"—see 1 Corinthians 16:22) was the heart cry of the early church. This mantra pointed to their eager anticipation of their King (Revelation 22:20).

If you are a ministry leader, I would encourage you to undertake a similar study and write an imprint statement for your organization. Having an imprint statement, in addition to mission and vision statements, helps us to describe and strive for a culture and ethos that embody Jesus for those we serve.

However, this is not just for ministry leaders. It's important that we all pay close attention to how we do what we do in our discipleship. Whether in the context of our organization, our home, our workplace, or our neighborhood, we are—in a sense—mirroring Jesus as we prepare people to be with Jesus. An imprint statement guides us to be with people as Jesus would be with them.

FOR DISCUSSION

———— + ————

Chapter One: Two Words That Will Change Your Life

1. Imagine yourself as a disciple of Jesus after his crucifixion. Suddenly, Jesus appears to you and leads you in a Bible study. How is this different from any other Bible study? What about Jesus' presence makes following Jesus more dynamic?

2. Have you ever wished you had been one of the original disciples? Why? How does the idea that Jesus himself is here to disciple you today change the way you think about your discipleship?

3. Why do you think it's so easy to slip into following programs for discipleship rather than following Jesus?

4. Did you pray the prayer at the end of the chapter? What was that like? What have you found helpful to remind you to keep an eye out for Jesus?

Chapter Two: The Discipleship Myth

1. What was the first part of the Bible you remember reading? Why did you read that section first? What stuck with you when you read it?

2. What's the problem with seeing Jesus as a model for discipleship?

3. Which of the roles in a fellow believer's life—mother, father, coach, peer—is most appealing to you? How does Jesus fulfill this role for you?

Chapter Three: Embracing Jesus as Your Pastor

1. How would you describe the difference between a pastor of a church and the pastoral role Jesus wants to play in your life?

2. How does Jesus' divine knowledge of you at your core make him particularly effective at pastoring you?

3. How is your discipleship changed by thinking about what Jesus is doing and saying as opposed to what he did and said?

Chapter Four: Choosing Jesus as Your Teacher

1. When have you been particularly stirred by a sermon or a reading of Scripture? What made the difference?

2. What has Jesus been teaching you lately? Where have you noticed lessons from Jesus coming to you?

3. We become like our teachers. Who are some of the people you find yourself resembling? What can you do to allow Jesus' teaching to come through more powerfully in your life?

4. What would you like Jesus to teach you?

Chapter Five: Learning to Pray in the Spirit

1. What do you find personally significant in the truth that you are a temple of the Holy Spirit?

2. What patterns of rest have you built into your life?

3. What practices have you found helpful to surrender to the leadership of the Holy Spirit? How does your imagination factor into your discipleship?

4. How long do you wait for the Holy Spirit to engage you in prayer before you get antsy? What helps you continue to wait?

Chapter Six: Joining the Great Co-Mission

1. Who has God placed in your life to assist you in your walk with him? How have they enriched your discipleship?

2. When you've considered the great commission—"go and make disciples of all nations"—in the past, how have you reacted? Have you found it intimidating? Empowering? Confusing? Why?

3. How does the idea of bringing people to Jesus to be discipled by him (not you or your church) change the great commission for you?

4. Which of the characteristics of Jesus and the early church—worship-driven, Spirit-led, prayer-dependent, grace-centered, Kingdom-obsessed—do you find to be most natural to you? Which do you think Jesus wants to grow you in?

Chapter Seven: Preparing People to Be Discipled by Jesus

1. How do you react to the idea that the vast majority of Christians aren't ready to be discipled by Jesus? In what ways do you feel "unready" to be discipled by Jesus?

2. How would you prepare someone for Jesus to give them their cross? As you reflect on your life, what are some crosses that Jesus has given you?

3. How would you explain the relationship of obedience to Jesus' commands and love of Jesus? How does obedience to Jesus' commands prepare us to be discipled by him?

Chapter Eight: The Ultimate Goal of Discipleship

1. How does remembering that Jesus has sent you into your context change the way you engage the people in your life?

2. What scares you about asking Jesus, "Where do you want me to go?" What excites you about the question? How prepared are you to go wherever Jesus sends you?

3. When was the last time you asked Jesus, "Why am I here?" What aspects of your life today do you need to ask Jesus about?

NOTES

—— ✚ ——

INTRODUCTION: THE COMING REFORMATION IN DISCIPLESHIP

1. John B. Watson, quoted in Deborah Blum, *Love at Goon Park: Harry Harlow and the Science of Affection* (New York: Basic Books, 2011), 130.
2. Blum, *Love at Goon Park*, 51.
3. Blum, *Love at Goon Park*, 51–52.
4. Blum, *Love at Goon Park*, 52.
5. Blum, *Love at Goon Park*, 222.
6. Blum, *Love at Goon Park*, 222.
7. Skye Jethani, *The Divine Commodity: Discovering a Faith beyond Consumer Christianity* (Grand Rapids, MI: Zondervan, 2009), 10.
8. Jethani, *The Divine Commodity*, 10.

CHAPTER 1: TWO WORDS THAT WILL CHANGE YOUR LIFE

1. It is worth noting that they weren't the only ones to not immediately recognize Jesus in his post-resurrection body.
2. Zechariah 11:12-13; Jeremiah 19:1-13; 32:6-9; Matthew 27:9; Exodus 12:46; Numbers 9:12; Psalm 34:20; John 19:36.
3. Dietrich Bonhoeffer, *The Cost of Discipleship* (New York: Collier Books, 1963), 63–64.
4. Bonhoeffer, *Cost of Discipleship*, 64.
5. Luke Timothy Johnson, *Living Jesus: Learning the Heart of the Gospel* (New York: HarperOne, 1999), 3.
6. Johnson, *Living Jesus*, 4–5.

CHAPTER 2: THE DISCIPLESHIP MYTH

1. Robert Gelinas, *The Mercy Prayer: The One Prayer Jesus Always Answers* (Nashville: Thomas Nelson, 2013).

2. John Eldredge, *Fathered by God: Learning What Your Dad Could Never Teach You* (Nashville: Thomas Nelson, 2009), 27.

3. Dallas Willard, *Discipleship*, quoted in Bill Hull, *Conversion & Discipleship: You Can't Have One without the Other* (Grand Rapids, MI: Zondervan, 2016), 20.

4. Dallas Willard, *The Great Omission: Reclaiming Jesus's Essential Teachings on Discipleship* (New York: HarperOne, 2006), 4.

5. Willard, *The Great Omission*, xiv.

6. Skye Jethani, *With: Reimagining the Way You Relate to God* (Nashville: Thomas Nelson, 2011), 14.

7. Kenneth Boa, *Conformed to His Image: Biblical and Practical Approaches to Spiritual Formation* (Grand Rapids, MI: Zondervan, 2001), 372.

8. Boa, *Conformed to His Image*, 373.

9. Bobby Harrington and Jim Putman, *Discipleshift: Five Steps that Help Your Church to Make Disciples Who Make Disciples* (Grand Rapids, MI: Zondervan, 2013), 118.

10. As recorded in James H. Cone, *Risks of Faith: The Emergence of a Black Theology of Liberation, 1968–1998* (Boston: Beacon, 2000), 61.

11. Cone, *Risks of Faith*, 61.

12. King wrote and spoke about this experience often. See *Stride Toward Freedom: The Montgomery Story* (New York: Harper & Row, 1958); *Strength to Love* (reprint, Philadelphia: Fortress, 1981); "Thou Fool," sermon given August 27, 1967, at Mt. Pisgah Baptist Church.

CHAPTER 3: EMBRACING JESUS AS YOUR PASTOR

1. Dallas Willard, *In Search of Guidance: Developing a Conversational Relationship with God* (San Francisco: HarperSanFrancisco, 1993), 112. This book was later expanded and republished as *Hearing God: Developing a Conversational Relationship with God*.

2. Genesis 16:7-14; Exodus 3:2; Joshua 5:13-15; Judges 5:23; 13:9-22; 2 Kings 19:35; Zechariah 1:12.

3. Indeed, many scholars believe that the angel of the Lord was preincarnate appearances of Jesus. For a full treatment of the subject, see Ron Rhodes, *Christ Before the Manger: The Life and Times of the Preincarnate Christ* (Grand Rapids, MI: Baker, 1992).

4. Or "One Who Wrestles with God."

5. Jeff Johnson, "Season 2, Episode 5: Clara Brown," August 15, 2016, produced by Delve Denver, podcast, MP3 audio, 40:39, http://www.delvedenver.org/?p=275. Also see "Clara Brown," Colorado Women's Hall of Fame, accessed December 11, 2017, http://www.cogreatwomen.org/project/clara-brown/.

CHAPTER 4: CHOOSING JESUS AS YOUR TEACHER

1. See Robert A. Guelich, *The Sermon on the Mount: A Foundation for Understanding* (Dallas: Word, 1982).

2. We have two versions of the same sermon: Matthew 5–7 and Luke 6 and 12.

3. Dallas Willard, *The Spirit of the Disciplines: Understanding How God Changes Lives* (New York: Harper & Row, 1988), ix.

4. Willard, *Spirit of the Disciplines*, ix.

CHAPTER 5: LEARNING TO PRAY IN THE SPIRIT

1. A. W. Tozer, *The Pursuit of God* (Camp Hill, PA: Christian Publications, 1982), 17.

2. Gregory A. Boyd, *Seeing Is Believing: Experience Jesus through Imaginative Prayer* (Grand Rapids, MI: Baker, 2004), 56.

3. Boyd, *Seeing Is Believing*, 107.

4. Boyd, *Seeing Is Believing*, 72.

5. Boyd, *Seeing Is Believing*, 72.

6. Boyd, *Seeing Is Believing*, 112.

7. Boyd, *Seeing Is Believing*, 109.

8. Boyd, *Seeing Is Believing*, 116.

9. To learn more about Glen Eyrie, see gleneyrie.org.

CHAPTER 6: JOINING THE GREAT CO-MISSION

1. To find out more about this amazing man's life, see Charles M. Pepper, *Life-Work of Louis Klopsch: Romance of a Modern Knight of Mercy* (New York: GreggPress, 2008), 324–325. Also see "The Origins of the Red-Letter Bible," Crossway, posted March 23, 2006, accessed December 12, 2017, https://www.crossway.org/articles/red-letter-origin/.

2. See Acts 20:35; 22:17-18, 21; 23:11; 1 Corinthians 15:3; and 2 Corinthians 12:1-10.

3. Willard also opted for this interpretation in his book *The Great Omission: Reclaiming Jesus's Essential Teachings on Discipleship* (San Francisco: HarperOne, 2006), 5.

4. Robbie F. Castleman, "The Last Word: The Great Commission: Ecclesiology," *Themelios* 32, no. 3 (April 2007), 68–70, http://s3.amazonaws.com/tgc-documents/journal-issues/32.3_Castleman.pdf.

5. Joe Hutto, *Illumination in the Flatwoods: A Season with the Wild Turkey* (New York: Lyons Press, 1995), 19–20.

6. Eugene Peterson, *The Jesus Way: A Conversation on the Ways That Jesus Is the Way* (Grand Rapids, MI: Eerdmans, 2007).

7. Philip Yancey, *What's So Amazing about Grace?* (Grand Rapids, MI: Zondervan, 1997), 66.

CHAPTER 7: PREPARING PEOPLE TO BE DISCIPLED BY JESUS

1. In the Old Testament, there were actually three tithes: the tithe for the Priests and Levites (Numbers 18:21, 24); the Festival tithe (Deuteronomy 12:17-18; 14:23); and the tithe for the poor (Deuteronomy 14:28-29; 26:12-13). The first two tithes were annual and the latter was collected every three years. See Randy C. Alcorn, *Money, Possessions, and Eternity* (Carol Stream, IL: Tyndale, 1989), 213.

2. Robert Gelinas, *Finding the Groove: Composing a Jazz-Shaped Faith* (Grand Rapids, MI: Zondervan, 2009), 104.

3. Dietrich Bonhoeffer, *The Cost of Discipleship* (New York: MacMillan, 1963), 96.

4. Bonhoeffer, *Cost of Discipleship*, 99.

5. Reggie L. Williams, *Bonhoeffer's Black Jesus: Harlem Renaissance Theology and an Ethic of Resistance* (Waco, TX: Baylor University Press, 2014), 15.

6. Williams, *Bonhoeffer's Black Jesus*, 25.

7. Bonhoeffer, *Cost of Discipleship*, 99.

8. Bonhoeffer, *Cost of Discipleship*, 99.

9. I unpack these ideas in their entirety in my book *Living Sacrifice: The Cross as a Way of Life* (Aurora, CO: RGPress, 2015).

10. Gene Edwards, comp., *100 Days in the Secret Place* (Shippensburg, PA: Destiny Image, 2001), 20.

11. Jim Mullins, "1 Year Ago Today: A Bright Night for the Church: Love Your Neighbor Rally," reposted as blog on *Redemption Tempe*, May 29, 2016, http:// tempe.redemptionaz.com/1-year-ago-today-a-bright-night-for-the-church -love-your-neighbor-rally/. See also http://www.azcentral.com/story/news /local/phoenix/2015/05/29/law-enforcement-prepares-protest-outside-phoenix -mosque/28136557/ and https://news.vice.com/article/heres-what-happened -at-the-anti-islam-protest-and-draw-muhammad-contest-in-arizona.

12. I've included the categorized list in appendix A on page 149 of this book.

13. John 13:23; 19:26; 20:2; 21:7; 21:20.

14. James K. A. Smith, *You Are What You Love: The Spiritual Power of Habit* (Grand Rapids, MI: Brazos, 2016), 7.

15. Smith, *You Are What You Love*, 2.

CHAPTER 8: THE ULTIMATE GOAL OF DISCIPLESHIP

1. Daniel Taylor, *The Myth of Certainty: Trusting God, Asking Questions, Taking Risks* (Grand Rapids, MI: Zondervan, 1992), 29. I've interacted

with this idea from Daniel Taylor in my previous book *Finding the Groove: Composing a Jazz-Shaped Faith.*

2. Os Guinness, *The Call: Finding and Fulfilling the Central Purpose of Your Life* (Nashville: Word, 1998), 4.

3. Edith Margaret Clarkson, "So Send I You," *The Hymnal for Worship & Celebration* (Nashville: Word Music, 1986), 310.

4. Quoted from the NIV, 1984 version.

5. For more information, see project127.com.

6. Gelinas, *The Mercy Prayer.*

EPILOGUE: THE THIRTEENTH DISCIPLE

1. To explore Swanson's work for yourself, see http://johnaugustswanson.com.

2. Johnson, *Living Jesus*, 11.